The North American Securities Administrators Association
and
The Council of Better Business Bureaus, Inc.

How to be an
Informed
◆
Investor

Protect Your Money from
Schemes, Scams & Frauds

Mega-Books

A **BENJAMIN** BOOK

In memory of Ted Benjamin,
who brought intelligence and integrity
to all his business dealings

To Get Additional Copies
Single copies of this book are available from your local Better Business Bureau
(see Appendix A for addresses), or the Council of Better Business Bureaus,
4200 Wilson Boulevard, Arlington, VA 22203.

Special Discounts for Quantity Purchases
Special discounts for bulk quantities are offered to business firms, associations, government
agencies, and other organizations that plan to use this title as a promotional, educational,
or public relations tool. On orders of 2,500 or more copies, back cover identification and
message are available, subject to approval of CBBB and NASAA. Contact: Mega Books,
240 East 60th Street, New York, NY 10022. Telephone: (212) 355-6200.

Author: Virginia Schomp
Editor: Toni Ann Scaramuzzo
Project Manager-CBBB: Roger F. Campbell, Jr., Director & Executive Editor of Advertising,
  Business and Consumer Publications
Project Manager-NASAA: Karen L. Terhune, Chair, NASAA Investor Education Committee
Editorial Assistant: Molly Walsh
Designer: Drew Hires

97 98 99   10 9 8 7 6 5 4 3 2 1

Produced by: Mega-Books with The Benjamin Company, Inc.
240 East 60th Street
New York, NY 10022

Library of Congress Cataloging-in-Publication Data
  Schomp, Virginia
  How to be an informed investor: protect your money from schemes, scams & frauds / the North
  American Securities Administrators Association and the Council of Better Business Bureaus, Inc.,
  (author, Virginia Schomp).
  p. cp.
  Rev. ed. of: Investor Alert! / the North American Securities Administrators Association and the Council of
  Better Business Bureaus, Inc., (author, Wilbur Cross). ©1988
  Includes index
  ISBN 0–9657200–0–4 (alk. paper)
  1. Investments—Handbooks, manuals, etc. I. Cross, Wilbur. Investor Alert! II. North American Securities
  Administrators Association. III. Council of Better Business Bureaus. IV. Title. HG4527.C78 1997
  332.B—dc21   97-3348
                                                      CIP

ISBN 0–9657200–0–4

TABLE OF CONTENTS

Preface

Consumers lose hundreds of millions of dollars every year to investment fraud as it touches all segments of society: the rich and the poor, the young and the old. Not only does investment fraud cross over the border between America and Canada, but it also extends overseas. Swindlers and con artists prey on the hopes of us all. They will steal as readily from those in pursuit of the modest goal of financial security as from those who dream of great wealth. No one is immune.

Ignorance and greed are the allies of swindlers. Con artists know that many people generally do not understand what is being offered to them and hear only the promise that they can make a great deal of money easily and quickly by handing over their savings to the promoters.

Once the money is in the hands of the swindlers, it is usually gone for good. Even if these promoters are arrested and convicted, there is often nothing left to give back to the victims. Therefore, it is vitally important for investors to protect themselves before money changes hands.

Lured by the promises of high returns or huge tax savings, far too many investors plunge into fraudulent investments without first investigating them. The same scams are worked over and over again on people who do not take the time to check out the offers or learn the danger signs. The Better Business Bureaus (BBB) and the state securities administrators in the United States and Canada have seen this story repeated thousand of times.

Today even old schemes and scams are being perpetrated in the electronic marketplace via a new "medium", the Internet. A skillful and technologically adept fraud artist can create a Web page that appears so sophisticated and enticing that an investor assumes it must be legitimate.

The purpose of this book is to alert investors to the methods of operation, the typical pitches, and the danger signs of investment fraud in both the traditional and on-line marketplaces. The sponsors of this book are the North American Securities Administrators Association (NASAA), the organization of state officials who administer and enforce the securities laws at the grass roots level, and the Council of Better Business Bureaus (CBBB), the umbrella organization for the Better Business Bureaus in the United States and Canada.

Each year local BBBs distribute millions of company reports on business performance and hundreds of thousands of advisories, alerts, press releases, charity reports, and educational brochures offering information to consumers and businesses on how to avoid scams and make wise purchasing and investment decisions. The BBB Web page (**http://www.bbb.org**) also offers the same information to consumers and investors.

NASAA has two services enabling the speedy and efficient fulfillment of consumer requests for a variety of information. An automated, toll-free telephone information retrieval system (1-888-84-NASAA) gives callers easy access to prerecorded information. Consumers also can phone the toll-free number to order NASAA publications through a fax-back/voice mail system. There's also a compendium of investor education materials just a click away at NASAA's Internet site on the World Wide Web (**http://www.nasaa.org**).

This book does not attempt to tell the public how to invest their money, but rather to give them the tools to distinguish between legitimate and fraudulent investment opportunities and to choose those investments that may be appropriate for them. In today's traditional and electronic marketplaces, this is not an easy task.

With the deregulation of a large part of the financial market there has been a proliferation of investment vehicles that are complicated and baffling, even to experts. Con artists have been equally prolific in coming up with scams to fleece the investing public. Often it is very difficult to distinguish a legitimate investment opportunity from a scam. Nevertheless, investors are not defenseless. This book provides descriptions of old and new cons, cites examples of how investment schemes and scams work, offers ways of identifying potentially fraudulent deals, and gives details about related state, federal. and local enforcement activities. It is hoped that this advice will enable investors to protect themselves and avoid the costly lessons taught to thousands of Americans every year by fraudulent promoters who are ready, willing, and able to steal their money.

James L. Bast
President and CEO, CBBB

Mark J. Griffin
President, NASAA

Introduction

Investigate Before You Invest

Ponzi schemes, pyramid schemes, phony business opportunities—some tried-and-true scams—have been bilking unwary investors for ages. Other, newer schemes take advantage of trends such as investor interest in new technologies or operate through new media such as the Internet. Here is a quick look at some cons operated by swindlers who specialize in stealing from people who do not take the time to investigate before they invest.

- A Missouri stockbroker used his free evenings to tout his services through messages posted on a commercial on-line bulletin board. Under the alias "A GOOD TRADER," the broker lured customers with a number of dubious claims, in one case implying that a wealthy financier was a major behind-the-scenes player in the thinly traded stock of a tiny cruise line. In his on-line messages, the broker, who was not even licensed to do business in Missouri, invited unwary investors to assist in defrauding themselves by contacting his toll-free number or e-mail address.

- A California company used glossy sales charts projecting annual returns of $23,530 for purchasers of a $10,000 interest in a 900-number pay-per-call service. "Limited partnerships" were sold with the assurance that the company already had "300 lines . . . set up throughout the U.S." and that investments were "backed by a U.S. Treasury bond that secures their principal 100%." In fact, there *were* no lines, and all the funds were siphoned off to pay for sales commissions and expenses. One victim of this scheme: a seventy-eight-year-old woman whom the company threatened to sue when she refused to increase her investment.

• A Colorado man invested $20,000 in a business opportunity scheme based on fund-raising among nonprofit organizations and schools. The investment included a protected territory for the business plus 25,000 coupon books offering two-for-one savings on popular consumer items. With the promise of complete support and assistance in signing up distributors to work under him in bringing this new business to Colorado, the man anticipated a six-figure income. Instead, he discovered that the business was *not* new to his state, that the company was signing distributors in direct competition to him, and that the product was not marketable. When he filed a lawsuit for fraud in Colorado, it was thrown out because the company was based outside the state. He lost his entire investment.

• Six hundred investors in Arkansas and California lost $10 million to a promoter who promised them a no-risk 36 percent annual return in U.S. Treasury bills. The con artist, a former preacher and Sunday school teacher, targeted his scheme at religious individuals who believed they were dealing with a man blessed with extraordinary business abilities. Early profits seemed to support their belief in this classic Ponzi scheme—the promoter paid handsome dividends to initial investors, using money raised from new victims.

• Victims targeted by an Atlanta company operating a recovery room telemarketing scam found out that lightning can indeed strike twice. First, these unwary consumers were taken in by a scheme operated by two New York firms offering fraudulent license application services. Promising high earnings and low risk, the firms charged $7,000 to obtain specialized mobile radio (SMR) licenses—licenses that the investors could have obtained for $200 by applying directly to the government. Then the Atlanta operation stepped in, falsely promising to help defrauded investors recover their losses and find buyers for their SMR licenses, in exchange for an upfront fee. In fact, the victims of this "double scamming" *did* recover a portion of their investment—when a federal district court judge ordered both the New York and Atlanta scammers to cease operations and pay a total of nearly $200,000 in consumer restitution.

Investor's Checklist

Being a wise investor means taking the time to examine each investment before signing on the dotted line. Here is a checklist of questions that can serve as a starting point when you consider an investment. If you answer "yes" to most of these questions, the investment may be suitable for you. If most of your checkmarks are in the "no" column, be cautious about proceeding.

Yes	No	
		Does the investment meet your personal investment goals?
		Are the claims made for the investment realistic?
		Do you understand and accept the risks involved in the investment?
		Is the investment part of a balanced portfolio?
		Can you sell the investment when you want to?
		Do you understand and accept the conditions that apply if you withdraw from the investment?
		Has the seller given you written information that fully explains the investment?
		Have you read (and understood) the information?

Becoming an Informed Investor

Whether you are the target of an old-style con, one of the new generation of high-tech swindles, or an old scam dressed up in modern clothing, you need not become yet another victim. Often a little research, a single phone call, or a brief letter of inquiry can alert you to a financial disaster in the making, in time for you to avoid becoming a casualty. Hundreds of brochures, books, video and audio cassettes, and on-line computer services offer information on investing basics, including how to avoid frauds and scams, read and understand account statements, and identify unauthorized transactions. A number of associations and state and federal agencies also provide education materials and answer specific investor queries. You will find addresses and phone numbers for many of these organizations listed in Appendix C.

Better Business Bureaus in the United States and Canada answer inquiries on companies located in the areas they serve. It is a good idea to contact your local Better Business Bureau for a reliability report on any company in which you are considering an investment. The BBB system offers BBBOnLine, an Internet service to help consumers distinguish legitimate on-line offers from scams. See Appendix A for listings of BBB offices. For information on BBB on-line programs, see "BBB and NASAA On-line" in chapter 10, "On-Line Investment Fraud."

Your state securities agency cannot tell you *how* to invest, but it can help you investigate the risks and related rewards of specific investment products. For information on the North American Securities Administrators Association's (NASAA's) toll-free telephone information retrieval system and Internet site on the World Wide Web, see "BBB and NASAA On-Line" in chapter 10. You also can contact your state securities agency, listed in Appendix B, for answers to these questions:

- Is the promoter of an investment opportunity registered/licensed to sell securities in your state?
- Has written information that you received about the investment been filed in your state?

• Does the investment comply with your state's securities laws?

Finally, to help investors anticipate frauds, scams, swindles, and other money-related threats, state securities agencies and the Better Business Bureaus offer the following ten cautionary guidelines, which should be heeded no matter what form of investment you are considering.

Ten Do's and Don'ts for Investors

1. Be wary of unexpected phone calls, letters, e-mails, or personal visits from strangers who offer quick-profit schemes that require an immediate investment.

2. Look with doubt on promises that you can "double your money" or expect some other high return on your investment within a short period of time.

3. Turn down money requests accompanied by high-pressure warnings such as "Tomorrow will be too late" or "Act now because there will soon be a long waiting list of others who want to take advantage of this golden opportunity."

4. Always demand *written* information about the organization behind the investment plan and its track record. Bear in mind, though, that printed documents can easily be created, forged, or falsified.

5. Be suspicious of claims of "inside information," hot tips, and rumors that supposedly will give you a big advantage over other, less knowledgeable investors.

6. Ask for a prospectus, offering circular, financial statement, or similar document before you consider investing. Then read the small

print carefully and make sure you understand the terms thoroughly before signing any kind of commitment.

7. Before making a commitment, get a professional opinion from your attorney, stockbroker, accountant, or other reliable consultant.

8. Contact your local Better Business Bureau to determine whether there have been any previous inquiries or complaints about the company. Request a reliability report on the firm. Whenever possible, deal with established businesses whose reputations are known and respected in their communities.

9. Check with your state securities administrator and other appropriate government agencies to confirm that the company or individual is properly licensed to conduct the business in question and whether there have been any previous violations of the law.

10. When in doubt, make no promises or commitments, no matter how tentative. It is far better to wait and lose an opportunity than to take the plunge and lose everything. When hounded on the phone by an aggressive promoter, do not be afraid to hang up without explanation. You do not owe the caller anything. In fact, this kind of solicitation is an invasion of your privacy, and may be a violation of federal law.

Chapter 1

Business Opportunity Schemes

The opportunity to invest in a franchise seemed to be exactly what Carol and Allen were looking for—a chance to break out of the endless commuting rat race and gradually establish a business that they could operate out of their own home. All they had to do was invest $4,000 in an initial supply of a brand-new window-washing compound that left glass crystal-clear and unstreaked. The investment guaranteed "an exclusive territory, sales literature, and participation in a forthcoming national ad campaign that [would] quickly make the product a 'best-seller.' "

At first skeptical when they received a "cold" telephone call, Allen and Carol were quickly convinced after the stranger at the other end of the line talked them into letting him pay a visit, during which he demonstrated the "space-age" product (which he said was used to clean portholes and instruments in spacecraft) and displayed advance proofs from the advertising program. As he explained it, the couple would not even have to store or process their supply of the washing fluid. It would be kept safe and sealed in containers in the company warehouse. All they had to do was take orders from local supermarkets and hardware stores, maintain the books, and collect the payments. The deluge of orders would follow as soon as the ad campaign started to run and store buyers spotted their names as product distributors in their area.

What the young couple particularly liked about the plan was that they could begin in a modest way, continue with their jobs, and then phase into their own business when they were ready to become full-time entrepreneurs. "If, for any reason, you find that you don't like the business," they were assured, "we can always find someone else to take over your territory and purchase the unsold supplies. After all, the liquid retains its strength in storage indefinitely, in sealed fifty-gallon drums. There is no depreciation."

Not only was there no depreciation, there was no supply. The warehouse receipts handed to Carol and Allen in return for their $4,000 were falsified copies of receipts for a single shipment of drums delivered to a warehouse in the name of the operators of the scheme—just enough to establish the necessary documentation. Other would-be entrepreneurs taken in by the scheme had received copies suitably altered for their eyes alone.

The operators of this swindle were later arrested and indicted for fraud, evidenced by their having few supplies, no advertising contracts, and no evidence that they intended to develop even the most rudimentary window-cleaning supply business. By that time, however, the money taken from distributors-to-be had largely vanished. Carol and Allen, along with many others who had been bilked, were unable to recoup any of their investment.

Both Sides of the Coin

More than eight million people in the United States earn income from legitimate franchise operations. The International Franchise Association, an industry watchdog group, estimates that franchises account for more than $800 billion annually in sales and almost 41 percent of all retail sales.

This abundance of business opportunities presents a bright array to would-be entrepreneurs who want the freedom to work on their own and to have more control over their lives than a standard employment arrangement allows. They can select their field of endeavor from an astonishing variety of businesses, ranging from the conventional to the exotic. They also can elect to do business in the privacy of their homes, converting once idle space into a beehive of productive activity.

Consider the case of Jerry and Carla, who were convinced they had discovered the formula that would solve their financial problems forever. It sounded like a clever idea—selling high-quality imitation jewelry under a franchise known as Fabulous Fakes. For $18,000, they were promised, they would receive the necessary display and store fixtures, professional counseling about starting and operating the business, and a substantial inventory of the jewelry, which featured the imitation diamond called cubic zirconia.

Martin Baum, a Fabulous Fakes executive, assured the couple that they could not possibly lose money on the venture. After all, they would get a full return on their investment just through discounts on future purchases to supplement their inventory as the merchandise was sold. Naively accepting these promises at face value, they committed their total savings of $8,000 and convinced Jerry's parents to lend them an additional $10,000.

Their investment purchased franchise rights in a town convenient to their home. Sure enough, they quickly had a going business as they began to sell their inventory of jewelry. Everything went smoothly for three months, until suddenly the requested shipments from the franchiser stopped. This seemed strange to the couple, since they had been sending

Warning Signs

Here are eight warning signs the BBB and NASAA advise potential investors to look for when you are considering making an investment in a franchise or other business venture.

1. ***Use of classified ads that urge prospects to call an 800 number.*** These types of ads often are come-on pitches designed to lure you into calling a high-pressure telemarketing boiler-room operation. Do not be deceived into thinking that the information in an ad is accurate or legitimate just because it appears in a reputable newspaper or magazine.

2. ***High-pressure sales tactics.*** Be wary of sales pitches, whether from individuals or in ads, that urge you to get in on the ground floor or to act at once. Shady promoters do not want you to take the time to read the small print, talk to others in the business, or visit facilities in person.

3. ***Wild and unsubstantiated claims about potential earnings.*** No honest business is built on quick, astronomical profits. Legitimate promoters will qualify their success stories and make it clear that profits depend on the dili-

gence and capabilities of the individual, not on some surefire sales plan or a product so superior to all others that it cannot fail to catch on.

4. ***Claims about "proven" concepts, no risk, or minimal risk.*** Going into business for yourself is inherently risky. No legitimate franchiser would ever assume the responsibility of underwriting franchisees who fail. Assurances that "you can't go wrong in this business" are a sure tip that you are being conned.

5. ***Unjustified start-up fees.*** If the job involves personal selling, there is no reason you should pay anything but a modest fee to cover literature, enrollment, and basic training. If products are involved, check out their value and make sure you are not paying outlandish prices, perhaps for inferior goods.

6. ***Evasive answers and lack of communication.*** A promoter's failure to provide details and a disclosure statement or to respond directly to inquiries should diminish your enthusiasm for any franchise or business venture. Evasive promoters may be hiding facts they do

not want you to know. Even if they are honest, this kind of weak communication can quickly erode any business in which communication and cooperation are vital.

7. *Reliance on references hand-picked by the promoter.* Peddlers of bogus business opportunities often rely on "singers"—people who are compensated for giving glowing testimonials. Singers may get paid for posing as satisfied business owners or they may be existing operators who are rewarded with additional goods and services for their high praise. Reputable business opportunity and franchise promoters will provide a list of current business operators, not just a few selected names.

8. *Tip-offs to fraudulent vending machine promotions.* These include:

   • *Location services* (unscrupulous vending machine promoters often claim that their company employs an expert locator to find prime locations for its machines; many times, this so-called expert has no experience with local vending conditions).

   • *"Good deals" on machines* (shady distributors falsely claiming to represent a vending machine manufacturer may sell defective machines for which repair parts are unavailable, or they may sell "bargain" machines at two or three times their actual value).

   • *Repurchase plans* (offers by vending promoters to buy back inventory from investors who no longer want to sell the products are seldom if ever workable).

   • *Restricted territories* (established vending machine manufacturers usually do not assign territorial franchises or rights; in some circumstances, territorial restrictions may even be illegal).

   • *Lease-back arrangements* (in some deals, purchasers have leased machines and then hired the seller to service them and collect the money, only to find that the cost of servicing is much greater than the funds collected).

   • *Packaging limitations* (machines that accommodate only merchandise that is packaged in a certain way limit the purchaser's purchasing and sale options).

payments, including, in many cases, deposits from customers who wanted to order items that were out of stock.

Annoyed but not really worried, Jerry phoned Martin Baum. The Fabulous Fakes executive was "on vacation." A follow-up phone call a week later elicited the news that Baum was now "out of the country." His assistant or some other accountable person? They were always away, ill, or in conference.

"We never got an answer from anyone," said Carla, describing the frustrations that finally led them to consult an attorney. They were advised to close the shop before they got into any further trouble with customers, but by that time there was little business to terminate.

Within a few months, Martin Baum was under investigation. He later was found guilty on four counts of fraud and four counts of selling unregistered franchises. Carla and Jerry and numerous other investors never received one cent of restitution.

Operation Missed Fortune

Business opportunity scams are not a new problem, but these swindles have skyrocketed in recent years. With the decline of traditional job security and the increase in job losses due to corporate downsizing, more and more consumers have looked to self-employment as a source of greater security or a second income. Always quick to seize on new ways to make an illicit buck, con artists have picked up on these changes in the job market.

In 1996, the Federal Trade Commission (FTC), NASAA, and other state enforcement officials conducted a massive crackdown on get-rich-quick employment schemes. **Operation Missed Fortune** targeted business opportunity scams including:

- A Florida-based pay telephone program that, for an initial investment of $12,756 to $41,320, sold investors pay phones, falsely claiming that they could earn annual income of as much as $28,560 per phone.

- A work-at-home "opportunity" promising that, for a fee of $38.95, consumers could earn $200 to $1,000 a week assembling products at home. All they actually received was a pamphlet with the names and addresses of companies offering work-at-home opportunities, many of which required the payment of additional fees for a start-up kit.

- A California company offering franchises for breathalyzers to be installed in vehicles driven by convicted drunk drivers. The company falsely promised that investors paying $30,000 could earn $288,648 per year from court referrals.

"When a business opportunity knocks," the FTC cautions, "consumers today have to take more than a quick look before opening the door and investing. It's not easy to examine an offer thoroughly, especially when firms use phony references and offer detailed charts showing likely earnings. But the extra legwork could prevent substantial losses."

Proceed With Caution

Typical fraudulent business opportunities involve vending machines, amusement games, pay telephones, and display racks for items such as greeting cards and CD-ROM computer software. Investigations show that business opportunity scams most often are promoted at trade shows and through small ads in the classified sections of newspapers and magazines. These scams also are increasingly promoted through high-pressure telemarketing tactics, and via on-line promotions and unsolicited e-mail messages.

Investors generally are promised instant riches. In one ad for a pay telephone scheme, the promoter promised, "Get 96 sites for $7,795. Then Retire!" In another case, a computerized medical billing venture promised consumers they could use their home computers to "earn up to $23,000 a year working only 28 minutes a day." Companies promoting pyramid schemes based on prepaid phone cards solicited investors through ads that read, "Would you spend $100 to generate $10,000 in less than 12 months?"

One Better Business Bureau reported that dissatisfied nine-to-five workers, retirees, and laid-off employees were among the many new entrepreneurs who were calling BBBs across the country to complain when their start-up ventures come to a quick and money-losing stop. In many cities, the Bureaus have seen a significant increase in people interested in starting their own businesses, the Bureau added, noting that there are still many people unemployed, and there are those with severance packages that they want to invest. Lured by false promises of big profits and easy work, the BBB said potential investors are getting caught in business opportunity schemes involving vending machines, invention marketing, and work-at-home promotions.

Investors lose tens of millions of dollars every year to flourishing business opportunity swindles. Individual losses range from a few hundred dollars for vending machine frauds to tens of thousands of dollars for ownerships of franchises that are nonexistent or shaky at best.

Victims of vending machine fraud, according to the BBB, who paid from a few hundred dollars to several thousand dollars for machines claim to have been misled about earnings, machine location, maintenance, and company support. They also found refunds were not easily obtainable and in some cases the company had just disappeared. "Investors think they can buy a vending machine, drop it off at a high-traffic location, sit back and watch the profits roll in. The truth is, legitimate vending machine enterprises, and other ethical business opportunities are not 'get-rich-quick' plans. They require knowledge and a full-time commitment."

Another trademark of the business opportunity scam is the promotion of an unproven product. A con artist touting a vending machine known as the "Alcohol Neutralizer" offered investors packages of five machines for $4,500. Installed in taverns and other places where liquor is served, the Alcohol Neutralizer would dispense an herbal pill containing an active ingredient that was claimed to reduce blood alcohol levels. Supposedly, the pills had been endorsed as safe and effective by the Food and Drug Administration (FDA) and were backed up by the work of Harvard Medical School researchers. In fact, the FDA had taken action to stop the manufacturing of the pills, and the researchers in question denied ever having produced supportive findings. An independent study by an Indiana University scientist found that the herbal ingredient in the pills might actually keep blood alcohol levels *higher* for a longer period than if the pill had never been taken.

Investors in fraudulent business opportunities often suffer major financial hardship. One victim in an FTC case lost more than $70,000; others have lost as much as $40,000 or more each. A Pennsylvania woman who responded to an advertisement for a pizza vending machine business opportunity was promised huge earnings and prime locations. Instead she lost her entire investment of $72,000. To make up for her losses, the woman and her husband were forced to mortgage their home and sell off a dairy cow herd. They are now working multiple jobs in a struggle to avoid losing their family farm.

Get the Facts on Franchises

The romance of going into business for oneself has captured the imagination of millions of people who are fed up with commuting, bored with nine-to-five office routines, are seeking extra income or job security, or who simply feel that a particular business has something new and fresh to offer. Legitimate business opportunities abound. Unfortunately, so do schemes sparked by the ingenuity and inventiveness of con artists.

To avoid falling victim to the ploys of these promoters, it is critical that you know your rights. Several states have laws requiring franchisers to provide prospective purchasers with detailed information about the business opportunity. In addition, a Federal Trade Commission rule requires that franchise opportunity promoters provide certain information to help you in your decision. Under the FTC Franchise Rule, "A franchise or business opportunity seller must give you a detailed disclosure document at least 10 business days before you pay any money or legally commit yourself to a purchase." This document must provide 20 specific items of information about the business, including:

- The names, addresses, and phone numbers of other purchasers.
- A fully audited financial statement of the seller.
- The credentials of the business's key executives.
- The cost required to start and maintain the business.
- The responsibilities you and the seller will have to each other once you go into business.

These tips from NASAA and the BBB will help prospective franchisees know what to look for and ask about before making an investment:

1. Make sure the seller of the franchise supplies you with a complete disclosure document and that you read it carefully. Pay particularly close attention to the portions dealing with risk, the business experience of the company and its directors, history of lawsuits, fees to be paid and conditions under which fees and deposits will be returned, audited financial statements for the previous three years, and substantiation for earnings claims. Also study carefully the estimate of initial expenses. If that estimate is too low, you may find yourself with insufficient cash to carry on until the business produces a cash flow.

2. Consult with an attorney, accountant, or other expert before paying any money or signing anything. Remember, you will be asked to pay a substantial sum of money, initially and during the course of the franchise relationship, and you will be committing yourself to a potentially long-term business relationship.

3. The experience of others is one of the most effective guides you

can use to determine how you are likely to do if you purchase a franchise. The disclosure document should contain the names and addresses of individuals currently operating franchises in the system. Contact at least five references and get the answers to these questions:

- Are you happy with your investment?
- Are you making the money you expected?
- Would you make the same investment again?
- Has the promoter come through for you?
- What do you like and dislike about the business opportunity?

4. Be on your guard against "singers" who are paid for their testimonials. If you are considering an investment in vending machines or rack displays, the best way to avoid phony references is to get the names and addresses of retail locations where the machines or displays are operating and visit them in person. You can then judge the quality and state of repair of the equipment and the traffic volume in the store.

5. Pay attention to the number of franchises terminated during the past three years—an unusually large number may be a danger sign. If there are no franchises, or very few, you will have no way of discovering from the experiences of others what you will be getting for your money.

6. Find out the number of hours and days per week you will be required to remain open and other rules the franchiser may have regarding the operation of the franchise. You may be unwilling or unable to work as many hours or days per week or per year as are required. Find out whether the franchiser has rules concerning

closing for illness, death, or vacation; the number of employees you will be required to hire, if any; or anything else. You may find some of these rules too restrictive and burdensome. Some will be found in the disclosure document, while others of a more detailed nature can be determined by questioning the franchise salesperson or broker with whom you are dealing.

7. Do not assume that promises of prime sites, exclusive territories, speedy repairs, and ongoing assistance will be kept. Remember that a con artist will promise anything to get your money. Many who get burned in business opportunities lose their money when promoters fail to come through with promised repairs and other ongoing assistance.

8. In franchising, widespread customer recognition of a trade name is the equivalent of goodwill. An unknown name means that you and each member of the franchise system will have to develop goodwill and recognition. As such, you will not be buying goodwill, which is a leading feature of franchise operations. If the name is unfamiliar to you and your friends, you should ask yourself whether you are getting your money's worth in buying the franchise.

9. Examine the site selection process outlined in the disclosure document. The location of a franchise is very important, and a poorly selected site will doom a franchise no matter how attractive its features. Determine what the franchiser will do to assist you in selecting an appropriate site and whether you will be able to change the site if it proves to be unsatisfactory. If the franchiser's participation in the site selection process appears to be perfunctory or if the franchiser offers no assistance, think twice about buying.

BUSINESS OPPORTUNITY SCHEMES

10. Training is one of the distinct advantages of franchising. It enables a franchise operator to acquire within a short time the skills an independent operator might take months or years to acquire. If the training described in the disclosure document is not sufficiently detailed, ask about it. Also ask existing franchise operators about the training they have received, including initial training and ongoing support as needed.

11. Check out the franchise with your local Better Business Bureau, consumer protection agency, state securities agency, or state attorney general. These organizations can tell you about the business's complaint history and its compliance with applicable state registration laws. Inquire about and examine their litigation history. An excessive number of claims against them may mean that they have not been performing their agreements.

Chapter 2

Investing in Commodity Futures Contracts

Ask someone outside the investment field what commodities trading is all about, and you might well hear a description of a crowded Wall Street trading floor with traders shouting hoarsely as they buy and sell soybeans, corn, industrial metals, and other economic staples.

These days that picture is only partly true to life. Markets in commodities and futures now are open to a much broader range of participants than the specialists who used to ply their trade in the trading pits of major commodities exchanges. As an investor, you can speculate on much more than what orange juice and pork bellies will cost two or three months from now. In addition to placing bets on produce from the surface of the earth and resources from beneath it, you can take a crack at estimating what foreign currencies, Treasury bills and bonds, and stock indices will be doing in the future.

Take the case of Marna and Peter, who had never invested in anything more exotic than the common stocks of blue-chip companies. "One day, when we were pulling together our income tax records and reviewing the rather trivial amount we had made on the stock market," said Marna, "we decided that something was wrong. Although we were happy that we would be claiming a tax refund, we also wished that we had been more adventure-some in the marketplace."

That was when, with the assistance of a Wall Street friend, they began to explore the areas of activity involved in futures markets and discovered that they could speculate on Treasury bond futures by trying to anticipate the fluctuations in interest rates. Another alternative was to trade in stock index futures and try to judge what the stock market would do over a period of several months. A third option was to invest in currency futures and specu-late on the rise and fall of the dollar. They decided that, win or lose, it would be worth the risk to set aside 20 percent of their investment funds and try to outguess the experts.

As their friend warned them from the beginning, the odds against success for amateurs were about ten to one. They would be treading on dangerous ground where they not only might lose their initial capital fast, but also could be held accountable for much more if their speculation backfired. In the end, they made the decision to trade through a managed fund account, realizing that they simply did not have the time or experience to make their own investment decisions. "Happily," reported Peter, "we had enough sense to place our chips in the hands of a manager whose fund had enjoyed a solid and well-documented track record over the past couple of years by pooling the contributions of many members and thus having sufficient resources. In one year, we made far more than we ever could have through conservative investments."

Despite their initial success, the couple decided not to increase their investment in futures, realizing that, even with the help of professionals, the next year's bottom line could be far less attractive. They also resisted the temptation to go it on their own and speculate directly, rather than through a fund. "We were scared off a bit," admitted Marna, "not only by some of the horror stories we had heard about scams and rip-offs in commodities but because we realized this field is risky even when you are dealing with an honest agent."

She was by no means being unduly cautious. As in most areas of investment where substantial profits can be made quickly, unscrupulous operators have set up shop and taken millions of dollars a year from unsuspecting investors in commodities and futures. In addition, they have been offering investment contracts or programs that look like futures contracts but are not traded on licensed futures exchanges. These con artists often prey on individuals who probably should not be investing in commodities futures, who do not understand the transactions, and who can ill afford the potential losses. It is not uncommon for even knowledgeable investors to become the victims of these very clever and convincing swindlers.

Fruitless Futures

The Delancey brothers are a case in point. They had established a small business wholesaling detergents in the Philadelphia area and were convinced that they knew a good thing when they saw it. With increasing demand for exotic fruits and vegetables in stores ranging from mom-and-pop groceries to giant supermarkets, markups were far above normal for papayas, mangoes, and other produce from the tropics and Asia. So the brothers were more than willing to listen to a "commodities expert from Hong Kong" who had come to the East Coast to sell futures contracts for a new strain of miniature bananas to be shipped in quantity from Macao to New York in three months. Its price would skyrocket as the delivery date neared and the product was promoted to consumers.

Investors' Bill of Rights: Commodities

This "Bill of Rights," prepared by the National Futures Association, the self-regulatory agency of the commodities industry, is designed to assist investors in making an informed decision before committing their funds.

Honesty in advertising

In practically every area of invest-ment activity, false or misleading advertising is against the law and subject to civil, criminal, and regula-tory penalties.

Full and accurate information

Before you make any investment, you have the right to seek and obtain information that accurately conveys all of the material facts about the investment and about the firm or individuals with whom you will be doing business.

Disclosure of risks

Unless your understanding of the ways you can lose money is equal to your understanding of the ways you can make money, do *not* invest!

Explanation of obligations and costs

You have the right to full disclosure of the obligations and costs involved in a given investment.

Time to consider

High-pressure sales tactics violate the spirit of the law. An investment that "absolutely has to be made right now" probably should not be made at all.

Responsible advice

Beware of someone who insists that a particular investment is "right" for you, especially if that person knows nothing about you.

Best effort management

Every firm and individual accepting investment funds from the public has an ethical and legal obligation to manage the money responsibly.

Complete and truthful accounting

It is your right to know where your money is and the current status and value of your account.

Access to your funds

In the absence of restrictions or limi-tations, you should be able to have access to your money within a rea-sonable period of time.

Recourse, if necessary

Your rights as an investor include the right to seek an appropriate remedy if you believe someone has dealt with you—or handled your investment—dishonestly or unfairly.

Knowing little about futures contracts, the Delanceys talked with a commodities broker who specialized in agricultural resources. It was a risky business, the broker informed them, and not for amateurs—not even for professionals, unless they could monitor the market daily and keep abreast of a very volatile field of trading. Still, the brothers felt somewhat heady about their "inside information" and the fact that they were aware of continuing consumer demands. The new banana crop could be a bonanza. So they handed a bank check for $10,000 to the Hong Kong trader as margin and made plans to realize their substantial profits when the time (not to mention the bananas) was ripe.

Unfortunately, the deal was as rotten as fruit long past its prime. The Hong Kong Commodities Exchange had no knowledge of the proposed shipments. The "trader" who had smilingly taken their money turned out to be an expert in con games, not commodities, and was nowhere to be found. And the Delancey brothers ended up poorer but certainly a lot wiser for their $10,000 seminar in high finance.

Inside the Commodity Futures Market

A commodity futures contract is an agreement to buy or sell a specified quantity of a commodity at a specified price in the future. Commodities include many different things—gold, silver, copper, sugar, coffee, soybeans, corn, wheat, foreign currencies, Treasury bills and bonds, stock indices, and more.

Commodity prices change rapidly, in response to many factors, including inflation, weather, strikes, economic forecasts and reports, new technology, politics, and foreign events. Because events affecting prices can take place at any moment, the financial risks of these investments are great. Another risk factor in commodity futures trading stems from the fact that a small amount of money (called the initial margin) controls a large quantity of the commodity. Even a small change in the commodity price can cause a large change in the value of the futures contract. An increase of a few cents in the price of a bushel of wheat, for example, can mean a large and rapid profit for the investor in wheat futures. A drop in price, on the other hand, can mean equally dramatic losses. Further, those potential losses are not limited to the original investment. In some cases, when prices drop, the investor may not only lose the initial margin but may be required to make additional margin payments.

In this volatile field of investments, it is particularly important to understand the risks and remain alert to the possibility of fraud. Fast-talking con artists often exaggerate your chances of making money, while minimizing the potential risks. Some red flags to watch for include unsolicited, high-pressure phone calls; claims of confidential, inside information; urgent advice that you must act at once; promises of huge, quick profits; and assurances that your investment is at virtually no risk. Also be wary of committing yourself to commodity instruments promoted as "fixed maturity contracts," "deferred delivery contracts," or "cash forward accounts," which are not traded through regulated commodities exchanges. These catchphrases are subtle ways of telling you that your cash is going to be tied up for a long, long time before you see any returns—if you ever do.

The Infallible Forecaster

From the files of the National Futures Association comes this example of the shrewdness of successful "shady traders."

Jim worked at a full-time day job, but with assets consisting of only a phone, patience, and an easy way of talking, he managed to turn a nighttime sideline into an ill-gotten fortune. His routine went like this: Jim would phone a potential victim and quickly assure that person that he was not asking for a cent. Instead, he only wanted to demonstrate his investment firm's research capabilities by sharing the forecast that a particular commodity was about to experience a significant price increase. Sure enough, the commodity price soon went up. A second phone call still did not solicit an investment. Jim simply shared another prediction, that the price of another commodity was about to go down. As predicted, the price soon declined. By the third phone call, the unwitting victim *insisted* on investing—with a sum large enough to make up for the opportunities already missed.

What Jim's phone contacts had no way of knowing was that this swindler had started out with a calling list of two hundred people. In the first call, he told one hundred people that the price of a certain commodity would go up and the other hundred that it would go down. When the price went up, he made a second call to the hundred who had been given the correct "forecast." Of these, fifty were told the next price move would be up and fifty that it would be down. Once the predicted price change occurred, Jim had a list of fifty people eager to invest—fifty people who handed this "infallible forecaster" half a million dollars from their savings accounts.

Questions to Ask Before Investing

Your first line of defense against investment swindles is to find out all you can about the transaction and the seller. The Commodity Futures Trading Commission, the federal government's commodities regulatory agency, advises investors to ask some hard questions before dealing with any firm selling commodities. Make sure the answers you receive are clear and understandable; evasive or incomplete answers should be regarded as warning signs.

Questions About the Seller
- *How did you get my name?*
- *Is there a well-known brokerage firm or bank that I can call for references concerning your firm?*
- *How long have you and your company been in business?*
- *How long have you been offering this particular contract or commodity?*
- *What specific services will you provide?*

- *When can I expect to receive your written disclosure documents?* These should include financial information about the firm and written copies of the representations that have been made to you.
- *Is your firm a member of the National Futures Association (NFA) and registered with the Commodity Futures Trading Commission (CFTC) or any other recognized regulatory agency?* Verify this information by phoning NFA's Information Center at 1-800-676-4632. Inquire about any disciplinary actions taken or customer complaints filed against the firm, its principals, or the salesperson. Also look into the employment background of the firm's principals and the salesperson and the disciplinary history of any registered firms with which they have been affiliated.

Questions About the Purchase

- *What will be the total cost to me?* Ask how much of the total cost will actually be used to purchase the commodity contract; how much will be taken out in commissions, fees, and other charges; when, how often, and how quickly you will have to send money; whether you will be subject to other costs and charges, such as storage or interest; how much you stand to lose; and whether you might have to pay more than the price quoted to you.
- *What is the current price on the open market for the commodity?* Ask where you can verify the seller's market quotes, and find out if these quotes are the same as those reported regularly on the commodity exchanges and in the newspapers.

Questions About the Market

- *Exactly how much does the market price have to move in my favor for me to get all of my money back and start making a profit?*
- *Do I lose all of my money if the market price stays the same or moves against me?* Also ask how much the market price would have to move

against you to cause the loss of all of your money.

- *What other liabilities am I assuming if I purchase this contract?*
- *How does this contract work?* Ask how you can get out of the market, how quickly you can cut your losses by getting out, and how quickly you can get your money if you make a profit.
- *Are transactions executed through a regulated commodities exchange?*

Questions About Safeguards

- *What kind of a written confirmation do I get when the purchase is made, and how quickly?* Insist on proof that the transaction has been executed through a regulated commodities exchange.
- *Where will the investment funds be held?* Ask if the firm keeps customers' monies separate from the firm's operating funds, and ask for the name and location of the bank holding customers' monies.

Both the CFTC and NFA have prepared informative brochures detailing risks, precautions, and opportunities of investing in commodities and futures. For ordering information, see Appendix C.

Chapter 3

Zeros, Junk Bonds, and Penny Stocks

A dealer in expensive recreational vehicles was enjoying a flush of prosperity, enticing prospective buyers by the hundreds with an advertising campaign running in local newspapers and airing on radio. The pitch is pretty well summed up by this typical headline:

FREE!
A $5,000 U.S. TREASURY BOND,
FULLY GUARANTEED
WITH YOUR PURCHASE OF ONE OF OUR NEW DELUXE LAND CRUISERS

Among the eager buyers was a would-be entrepreneur who tried to talk his friends into pooling their resources and forming a sales syndicate. "If we buy ten vehicles," he explained, "and sell them at a $2,000 discount—a pretty good incentive—we'll still end up with ten $5,000 bonds, or a profit of $30,000."

What the young man did not know was that the $5,000 represented the maturity value of the bonds *thirty years in the future* and that each was purchased by the dealer at only a fraction of its face value, $200 to be exact. Fortunately for him, as well as quite a few other prospective purchasers who might have acted too hastily, state securities regulators banned further advertising of this kind by the dealer as "false and misleading."

Zeros: Use and Abuse

Zero coupon bonds (zeros) are so named because the investor receives no (zero) periodic interest payments. Conventional, or coupon-bearing, bonds pay interest twice a year, with the interest rate determined by the coupon rate. For example, if you purchase a $5,000 ten-year bond with a coupon rate of 7 percent, you will receive $175 in interest twice yearly for ten years. Zeros, on the other hand, are set up to reinvest interest earnings at the same rate obtained at the time of purchase. Even though you receive no interest payments, you must still pay taxes each year on the accrued interest.

Zeros are issued by corporations, municipalities, federal agencies, and the U.S. Treasury. They may be marketed under a variety of names, including Treasury Receipts (TRs), Certificates of Accrual on Treasury Securities (CATs), and Treasury Investment Growth Receipts (TIGRs). Zeros vary widely in price, face amount, length of maturity, degree of risk, and yield. They are sold at a deep discount and are automatically locked in at a specific rate to achieve the stated yield. You can buy zeros for as low as 10 to 20 percent of their face value; a twenty-year bond could sell for as little as $1,000 per $5,000 face value. The farther away the maturity date, the lower the current selling price of the bond.

Although some states have restricted the use of zero coupon bonds as promotional devices, an unknown number of "zeros" still are used in sales campaigns for houses, cars, furniture, and other big-ticket items. These promotions are misleading, frequently failing to inform customers of the current value of the bonds, possible liquidity problems, tax consequences, and the susceptibility to interest rate fluctuations when zeros are redeemed prior to maturity.

Many investors are attracted to zero coupon bonds because they find security in knowing exactly what they will earn if they hold their bonds to maturity. It is wise to keep in mind that the price of a zero reacts significantly to interest rate changes. Generally when interest rates go up the bond prices go down; if interest rates go down then the bond prices go up. That means that the value of zeros is much more volatile than that of conventional coupon-paying bonds. If you must sell a zero coupon bond prior to maturity—and interest rates have risen since the time of purchase—your proceeds will be much less than they would have been if you had purchased a coupon-bearing bond of the same maturity.

State securities administrators caution that sales promotions based on zero coupon bonds often fail to inform customers of this disadvantageous situation, leading them to believe that they can make a huge profit any time they want to sell, because of the high face value of the instrument they purchased. As one state securities administrator summed up the problem: "The retailers know zero about 'zeros.' The customers know zero about 'zeros.' It's a nightmare situation for investor protection."

Be Informed About Zero Coupon Bonds

It pays to be wary when considering any type of major purchase that promotes a zero coupon bond as a bonus. Make sure you know or get the answers to the following questions.

- Can you see the prospectus of the company issuing the bond?
- Is this a high-risk offering from an issuer that may not be able to pay the face value when the bond reaches maturity?
- What are the present or future tax consequences of accepting the bond as a gift?
- What is the current market value—*not* the face value—of the bond offered, as paid by the promoter?

- For how much could you purchase the same bond through a reputable broker or bank?
- What is the resale market for the bond should you want to sell prior to maturity?
- What is the bond's rating?
- What, if any, call provisions apply?
- Could you make a better deal by purchasing a car (or whatever the item is) that carries some other type of incentive?
- Does your state have regulatory restrictions that make this kind of bonus offer illegal?

Penny Stock Fraud

Every year hundreds of thousands of investors become victims of promoters of fraudulent schemes involving penny stocks. Once a primarily regional phenomenon, penny stock fraud now exists nationwide and can be extreme-

Junk Bonds and Repos

Investors have incurred heavy financial losses of investments in "junk bonds." These high-yield, low-rated or nonrated bonds, often associated with corporate takeovers, became a popular area of investment in the mid-1980s. Thousands of individual investors were attracted to junk bonds because they seemed to offer the prospect of getting the highest returns around. Notwithstanding the high risks of some of these issues and the dramatic failure of others, investors often have seemed oblivious to the financial weaknesses of the bonds in which they choose to invest. Prospectuses for junk bond issues have carried warnings such as these:

- Based on current levels of operations and anticipated growth, the Company does not expect to be able to generate sufficient flow to make all the principal payments due on the Serial Senior Notes. . . .
- An investment in the Notes involves certain risks which prospective investors should carefully consider. . . . These risks include . . . the insufficiency of the Company's earnings to cover fixed charges. . . .
- Notes will be subordinated and unsecured and will not be entitled to the benefit of any guarantees, unlike most of the Company's senior indebtedness.
- The warnings, as required by law, are intended to give investors the

ly lucrative for promoters and equally costly for investors.

Penny stocks are low-priced securities, usually traded at under $5 per share in the over-the-counter (OTC) market, which is a network of securities and brokers who make transactions over the telephone. Many penny stocks are legitimate offerings, often issued by struggling young companies seeking to raise capital to begin or expand operations.

Abuse in penny stocks can stem from the fact that volume and price information on these securities is not automatically collected and made available to the public, as is the case with securities traded on a stock exchange. That can make it difficult or even impossible for an investor to obtain current penny stock prices. The National Quotation Bureau, Inc., located in New York City, prints a daily list known as the "pink sheets," which includes prices of particular OTC stocks, including some penny stocks. These sheets, which really are pink, must be purchased for a fee; brokerage firms generally are the only ones that can afford them.

information they need to make a sound decision. Yet it seems that some investors are willing to ignore these warnings in their search for high yields. Wise investors will ask their brokers for verified information on an issuing company's financial status. Another way to minimize risks is to invest in a junk bond fund, which owns hundreds of bonds from different issuing companies. Your broker or the bond fund's prospectus can provide information on the fund's track record.

- Another area of investment that has caused concern in past years is the sale of repurchase agreements, or "repos" (see p. 171). One of the largest securities frauds in history was a complex three-year scheme involving repos. Three officials of a large securities firm were convicted on criminal charges for selling government securities accompanied by agreements to later repurchase the securities by repaying the customers' purchase price plus interest. The firm claimed that it would hold the securities in safekeeping accounts on behalf of investors. Instead, it defrauded customers by selling them nonexistent securities or selling the same securities to more than one client. The plan unraveled when the firm began to use investors' funds to speculate in bond futures and other high-risk investments and lost heavily. In total, this repo scheme defrauded investors out of about $150 million.

The published prices for penny stocks are *not* necessarily the prices at which investors can sell their shares; for many penny stocks, no prices are published. Thus, in most cases, investors must rely solely on their brokers for price information. Fraudulent brokers take advantage of that fact to vastly overcharge investors, selling penny stocks with undisclosed markups of 100 percent or more. A customer may pay $2,500 for penny stocks without knowing that the broker may keep $1,250 or more on the transaction. A National Association of Securities Dealers' rule limits markups to 5 percent of a security's price. Unfortunately, this rule is not always followed by brokerage firms.

Another opportunity for abuse stems from the fact that many penny stocks are traded by only a few brokerage firms or even by a single firm. It can be a simple matter for a fraudulent broker dominating the market to manipulate a stock's price. A common ploy, often called "pump and dump," is for a brokerage firm to gather a large holding of a penny stock at a very low price. Through the use of high-pressure sales techniques, the firm's salespeople hype the stock and create demand, driving up the price. The price continues to rise until there are no more investors who will buy. At that point the bottom falls out, the price plummets, and investors are left holding worthless stock.

In an attempt to get more up-to-date prices for penny stocks, the National Association of Securities Dealers developed the Over-the-Counter Bulletin Board, an electronic system that allows eligible dealers to indicate prices twice daily. One by-product of the computer system has been the creation of competition among a stock's market makers. There has been an increase in the number of "firm" prices that must be honored when a broker calls to make a trade.

Many fraudulent penny stock investments are sold through unsolicited phone calls by boiler-room operators (see chapter 9). Using prepared scripts and high-pressure tactics, these con artists sell unsuitable investments, typically to unsophisticated investors who are clearly unsuitable candidates for risky penny stocks. Defrauded investors often include low-income seniors whose primary sources of income are Social Security payments and other retirement benefits. In many cases promoters have convinced clients to place IRA accounts in penny stock investments. In others they have sold penny stocks to customers without obtaining their agreement, and then billed those customers for purchases they never intended to make.

These tactics violate federal and state laws enacted to protect investors from fraudulent sales practices. Under a Securities and Exchange Commission (SEC) rule adopted in 1990, brokers must obtain financial information from a client in order to complete a written statement explaining why high-risk penny stocks are a suitable investment for him or her. Before selling a security, brokers must get the client's signature on the suitability statement as well as on a purchase authorization form. Many states have adopted similar rules.

Be Informed About Penny Stocks

If you decide to gamble on penny stocks, keep the following tips and precautions in mind.

- ✔ *Beware of unsolicited phone calls and salespeople who offer quick profits with little or no risk.* Do not fall for unrealistic promises of high returns, claims that the salesperson has "inside information" on a stock, or warnings that you must act quickly or miss out on a spectacular opportunity.

- ✔ *Check out the investment.* Ask the salesperson for a prospectus on the company whose shares are being offered and study this document for information on the history and management of the company, its financial status, risk factors, potential conflicts of interest, outstanding litigation, and plans for the use of investors' funds. You may be able to get additional information on a company through the SEC (see Appendix C) and your state securities administrator (see Appendix B). Check how many shares of stock will be or already have been transferred to principals or promoters at little or no cost. Also ask the salesperson for written copies of any research reports supporting predictions about the price of the stock or prospects for the company. Investigate the degree to which company products or services have been developed, tested, and proven useful. Be wary of investing if you are told that any of the information you request is unavailable or that there is no time to send it. By law, a broker is required to provide customers with a risk disclosure document prior to making any penny stock transaction. Regard as a red flag anything you read in the risk disclosure document, prospectus, or other documents that contradicts the salesperson's claims.

✔ *Check out the price.* Ask the salesperson what price you would receive if you wanted to sell the stock instead of buying it, and ask for the names of at least two other firms trading in the stock that you can call to verify those prices. Penny stocks do not each have a single price at which they are bought and sold. Instead, there are a number of different prices, including bid and ask prices. The "bid price" is how much someone is willing to pay for the stock; that is, the price at which you could sell your shares. The "ask price" is the price someone is willing to sell a security for, or how much you would have to pay. A large spread—the difference between the two prices—suggests that you may be at a serious disadvantage when you try to sell. Keep in mind that in a sizable portion of penny stock trades, the brokerage firm sells and buys stocks from its own inventory. Thus the firm can set the bid and ask prices to make money on the spread. It also profits from the markup—the percentage added to the selling price on top of the spread. Federal law requires penny stock brokers to disclose the bid and ask prices prior to engaging in trades.

✔ *Check out the broker.* See chapter 12, "How to Select and Work With a Stockbroker," for tips on investigating a broker's background and experience. Also be aware that brokers are required by law to disclose the amount of commission or compensation they receive in connection with a penny stock transaction.

✔ **Check out your alternatives.** If your broker's firm is the only one actively trading the stock, you will be dependent on that firm, even if you become dissatisfied with its performance.

✔ **Make sure you read the suitability statement and authorization form carefully.** Do not sign these documents unless they accurately reflect your investment needs and intentions.

✔ **Avoid "blind pools" and "blank checks."** These are investments in new companies that generally do not have any assets, employees, or stated business plan, other than at times to use the stock proceeds to buy an unspecified company or companies. A high percentage of these offerings are simply fraudulent vehicles for market price manipulation.

✔ **Remember that it is easy to invest in stocks that are being manipulated but often very difficult to sell them.** When a sales campaign designed to inflate stock prices ends, the price often plummets. Even investors with "paper profits" in fraudulent penny stocks can find it impossible to sell their shares and receive their "profits" and their original investment back. Your broker may try to talk you out of selling, refuse to execute your sell order unless you agree to invest the proceeds in other penny stocks, or simply stop taking your calls.

✔ **If you can not afford to lose your money, do not put it in penny stocks or other high-risk investments.** Remember that even investments in legitimate penny stocks are highly speculative, with the great majority of investors losing some or all of their money.

Chapter 4

High-Tech Scams

The 1990s saw rapid advances in the technology of the "information superhighway"—along with an equally rapid response by con artists eager to exploit the public's enthusiasm for high technology. According to the Federal Trade Commission (FTC), investment schemes involving high technology and Federal Communications Commission (FCC) licenses have already cost consumers hundreds of millions of dollars. With swindlers quick to take advantage of emerging technologies, the outlook for unwary investors is not bright.

Fortunately, there are steps you can take to avoid high-tech scams. The first is to understand how the federal government awards market licenses for new technology and how scam artists turn that process into a vehicle for fraud and abuse.

Telemarketing Complaint System
FCC LICENSE COMPLAINTS

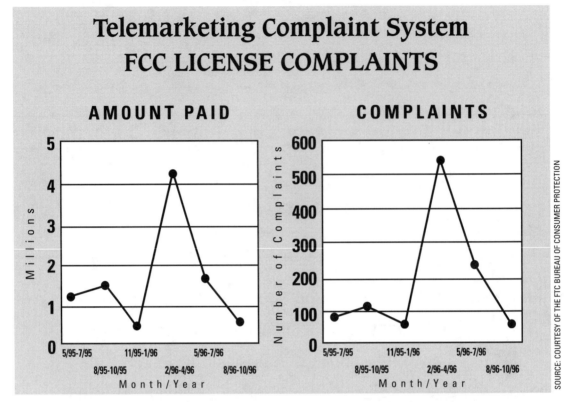

AMOUNT PAID   COMPLAINTS

SOURCE: COURTESY OF THE FTC BUREAU OF CONSUMER PROTECTION

FCC Licenses, Lotteries and Auctions

The FCC is responsible for granting licenses to individuals and entities interested in providing telecommunications services to the public. These licenses grant permission to use the radio frequencies in a given area. Typically, persons seeking licenses must fill out a long, complex application form, including detailed engineering and interference studies. Currently in some cases, licenses are sold by auction to qualified buyers. In others, it is "first in, wins." That is, the first individual or company to identify a market and submit a properly completed application is awarded a "conditional" license. After further scrutiny, the FCC may grant a "certificate of completion," allowing the applicant to begin operations.

In the past if the FCC received more than one application for a license in a single market, it sometimes held a lottery, which gave all qualified applicants an equal chance to "win" the license. Sometimes all the parties interested in a specific market formed a settlement group, or alliance, agreeing to share the license. In that case, if the FCC acknowledged the settlement as valid, the lottery for the market was suspended and the conditional license was awarded to the parties involved in the settlement.

While the FCC lottery process itself was not fraudulent or misleading, con artists seized upon it as a vehicle for investment scams. Many of these scams revolve around license application services, also known as application mills. Scam artists running an application mill offered to help consumers prepare an application to win an FCC license. They sometimes charged thousands of dollars for this "golden opportunity," even though, in most cases, the actual FCC application fee was a fraction of that amount. And they often claimed that investors could make enormous profits simply by reselling or leasing their licenses to one of the many deep-pocketed telecommunications companies.

The reality is quite different. Legitimate telecommunications companies typically applied for licenses themselves; they do not buy or lease licenses owned by individuals or partnerships. In fact, under some circumstances, leasing or selling arrangements can violate FCC rules and lead to the loss of the license. Other risks undisclosed by application mill promoters include:

- *Inflated claims.* Con artists vastly overstate the profits and understate the risks involved in investing in new high-tech ventures. In fact, high tech carries high risks—including the very likely prospect that investors will lose every penny of their capital.
- *Closed markets.* The average investor has no way of knowing whether the FCC, after receiving an eligible application for a license in a given market, has stopped taking applications for that market. Mills may continue to churn out applications for a closed market— and pocket investors' payments for filing those applications.
- *Spotty markets.* In many cases, licenses for developing a particular technology in major metropolitan markets are already owned by

legitimate telecommunications companies. The licenses that were available through the lottery process may be in rural markets where industry interest has been spotty, further reducing the investor's prospects of reselling at a profit.

- *Invalid licenses.* Licenses awarded for developing a communications system in a given market were automatically invalidated if "buildout," or construction of the system, was not completed within a specified period of time, usually one year. When a license was invalidated, the investor who hoped to resell it ended up with little more than a useless piece of paper. Further, participants in a lottery settlement, in which interest in a license was divided among a number of investors, could lose their licenses if the FCC uncovered errors made by the application mill that promoted the settlement process.

- *Poor odds.* It is far from certain that a lottery winner will have advanced from the conditional license stage to the final certificate of completion. In one year, the FCC estimated, only about one in ten applicants who won conditional licenses progressed to the stage where operations legally could begin.

The Take on High Tech

In the 1980s application mills largely focused on the FCC's cellular telephone license lotteries. Scams of choice in the 1990s have involved wireless cable television and other hot technologies. It is important to recognize that these technologies themselves are legitimate; it is the schemers exploiting them who cause problems.

Here is a look at some of the major technologies latched onto by promoters of high-tech investment schemes.

Wireless Cable Television

Wireless cable TV stations use microwave technology to relay cable television programs to rooftop antennas at the homes of subscribers. In 1983 the FCC opened filing for wireless cable licenses in major metropolitan areas for one day only and received more than 16,000 applications. In 1988, when a second-round lottery began for licenses in smaller, predominantly rural markets, the FCC was again flooded with a record number of applications.

This torrent was largely due to the speculative fever whipped up by the pie-in-the-sky sales pitches of a growing number of application mills. Con artists touting wireless cable TV as "the best-kept investment secret in telecommunications" and "television's last frontier" assured investors that they could make a lot of money with very little financial risk. One Bismarck, North Dakota, couple got a "cold" call from a telemarketing operator who explained that a $5,000 investment in a wireless cable application would yield a $2,500 monthly income within the first year of operation. A Nevada-based firm claimed to have devised a means by which investors, in exchange for a fee of $6,400, had sixty-five out of sixty-six chances of winning an FCC license. The salesperson for another company told prospective investors, "There's no financial risk. You put down $6,450 and you can get back $21,000 a year for the rest of your life."

What none of these con artists told their victims was that, although wireless cable TV is a legitimate industry, investing in it carries substantial risks. According to a Securities and Exchange Commission estimate, consumers invest half a billion dollars a year in wireless cable licenses that end up being worthless. Keep the following points in mind if you are considering an investment in wireless cable TV.

- Licenses for most of the major markets for wireless cable TV were awarded in 1983. As of 1992, the FCC had frozen the filing of all wireless applications for remaining markets. It is not known when the lottery will resume.
- Two licenses are awarded for each market area, and each license permits usage of only four channels out of a possible thirty-three. That means wireless cable TV systems must compete with other wireless systems in the same market, as well as with conventional cable and TV stations and home satellite dishes.

- Wireless cable TV has limitations. It can cost millions of dollars to develop a large, economically viable system offering subscribers an assortment of channels. Also, because the signal requires largely unobstructed transmission, it is unsuitable for areas with obstacles such as hills, trees, and buildings. While some wireless systems—particularly in flat, remote rural areas—have been successful, others have faltered.

- It may be difficult or impossible to secure financing to construct and operate a wireless cable station, and there may be no buyers for the station once it is operational.

Unscrupulous promoters have added a new wrinkle to wireless cable TV scams. Claiming that they already have the necessary FCC licenses, these con artists sell shares in a "general partnership" or "limited liability company" to buildout and develop the system. In many cases, the salespeople for these "postlottery" schemes misrepresent the number of licenses they hold, the number of channels needed for a commercially viable system, their qualifications for developing and running a wireless cable system, and/or the amount of investment capital required to fully develop the system. In one case, the FTC alleged that telemarketers had sold partnership interests in a wireless cable TV system for $7,500 to $20,000 each, promising investors a return of more than 35 percent a year. One year later the investors, who had forked over a total of $7 million, had not realized *any* return and, in fact, were informed that additional investments were required to keep the system going.

Specialized Mobile Radio

Another fast-growing scheme of the 1990s has involved the promotion of specialized mobile radio (SMR) as a competitor to cellular telephone service. SMR refers to a set of dedicated radio frequencies or channels. These frequencies are allocated by the FCC primarily to transmit and receive paging, data communications, and voice transmission, such as that used by taxis, delivery services, and other dispatchers. Claiming that an investment in an SMR network offers high returns and low risks, con artists induce consumers to invest thousands of dollars to purchase an SMR license. In truth, investments in SMR systems are extremely risky, and individuals can apply for a license directly from the FCC for as little as $250. Granted on a "first-come, first-served" basis, SMR licenses are readily available in many areas of the country.

In a related scheme, fraudulent brokers contact investors who already own an SMR license and offer their "expert" services in locating a company to buy or lease the license. Unwary investors pay a nonrefundable listing fee in advance. In many cases the broker simply pockets the fee, without even attempting to find a buyer. In still another twist on the SMR scheme, promoters solicit consumers to invest in partnerships to develop a network of SMR systems. Some scammers have roped in investors by projecting returns as high as several thousand dollars a year within eighteen months of start-up.

The key fact to keep in mind when contacted by someone touting the tremendous profit potential in SMR is that this new technology is still largely a dream. The single- and five-channel blocks typically promoted by swindlers simply do not accommodate enough telephone traffic to allow competition with cellular phone systems. In order to have enough transmission capacity to compete with cell phones, a conventional SMR system must be combined with other SMR systems into a network and must be upgraded with advanced digital equipment that can cost several million dollars. Once an SMR license has been granted, the system must be constructed within one year or the license expires. And until the system is constructed, the FCC prohibits the sale or lease of an SMR license to a third party.

Paging License Scams

Promoters of these high-tech scams offer to secure licenses covering a paging frequency in a major U.S. market. Investors are conned into paying between $1,000 and $12,000 per license, with the promise that they will easily be able to resell or lease their licenses to large companies eager to provide profitable two-way paging services to the public. Profit projections range from $1,000 a month to several hundred thousand dollars over the long term. One company sold multiple pager licenses at $1,580 to $2,900 each, assuring investors that they would realize a "safe" three-to-one return in just two years. The high-pressure sales pitch included warnings that prospective customers should "decide and move quick" because in a few days the company would "no longer be receiving applications." Telemarketers for another operation impressed investors with phone calls from the company's headquarters in the "World Trade Center." In reality, they were phoning from a boiler room in Broward County, Florida. Investors in this scheme were told to expect returns of "$1,000 a month." In other cases, fraudulent brokers have claimed an outstanding track record in helping paging license owners sell or lease their licenses to the corporate giants of the telecommunications industry.

Again, there is little or no truth in these scam promoters' claims. Paging

Project Roadblock

In 1996 the FTC and NASAA announced the results of a coordinated nationwide sweep of high-tech investment frauds built on emerging telecommunications systems. This massive crackdown yielded a total of eighty-five actions involving more than a quarter of a billion investment dollars.

Typical was the case of On-Line Communications, a license application service that made numerous misrepresentations in offering to obtain FCC paging licenses. Investors were told that paging licenses were scarce and highly sought after, making them an excellent low-risk investment. On Line charged $6,000 to $50,000 for its services, while neglecting to inform clients about FCC restrictions on the sale and lease of their licenses.

A settlement of the charges against one of On Line's principals prohibited him from acting as the director of any business engaged in telemarketing and from misrepresenting FCC regulations or the risks and profit potential of investment offerings.

licenses are an extremely speculative investment opportunity; while some licensees make money, most do not. Often licensees own frequencies that may allow only one-way paging or that must be shared with other licensees. If licensees try to develop their own systems, they may face stiff competition from established paging companies. And, as with SMR licenses, the FCC prohibits the assignment of a paging license to a third party through sale or leasing agreements until buildout of the system has been completed.

Interactive Video and Data Service (IVDS)

Licenses for wireless interactive television, or IVDS, cover a small sliver of the radio spectrum. This technology allows IVDS users to send responses to interactive TV programming such as polls, advertisements, and game shows. Unscrupulous promoters who extol the "limitless possibilities" of this relatively limited form of interactive television often falsely claim that IVDS can perform services such as providing "movies-on-demand," different camera angles for sports events, and various shopping opportunities. Some promoters claim to be putting together a general partnership or limited liability company to bid for and acquire IVDS licenses at FCC auctions. Others say they have already acquired a license and are selling interests in a partnership to develop a wireless interactive television system. As with all high-tech scams, investors are treated to projections of significant returns and little or no risk.

There is little risk, indeed, for the scam artist who funnels investors' funds into accounts labeled "commissions," "management fees," "operations," and "marketing." A promoter who raises $5 million by selling 1,000 partnership interests at $5,000 a piece may allot only $2 million for acquisition of the license and buildout of the system. Buildout and development of an IVDS system can cost millions of dollars per market. When sufficient funds are not set aside, investors often must make up the shortfall or risk forfeiture of the license to the FCC.

Most of the licenses for the country's top IVDS markets have already been issued, and licensees face strong competition from large, well-financed cable and telephone companies. In this volatile marketplace, the majority of licensees not only never realize astronomical returns but in fact end up losing some or all of their investment.

Pay-Per-Call 900-Number Scams

High-pressure salespeople selling partnership interests in a 900-number "information provider" service may offer glowing projections of 250 percent annual returns. What they do not offer is the information that four out of five 900-number ventures fail. Nor do they share details on the high costs information providers incur—costs that may include leasing special phone lines, paying for national promotion, and compensating endorsers used in advertisements. Four related California firms peddling partnership promotions in 900 numbers and other schemes took in $19.5 million in a year and a half. Eighty-five percent of those proceeds were siphoned off by the promoters. Investors were promised their money back in sixteen months and long-term profits of $70,000 or more; as of yet, they have not received a penny back.

Tips for Investments in High Tech

Big-time hustlers typically target small investors looking for an easy way to enhance their lifestyle or build their retirement nest egg. But even the most sophisticated investors have fallen prey to the swindlers' finely tuned sales pitches and professional-looking brochures, sales charts, and prospectuses. To avoid being taken, consumers must first be aware that con artists come in many disguises, promoting their schemes through a sophisticated array of telemarketing boiler-room pitches, seminars, direct mail and e-mail solicitations, program-length "infomercials," and other ads on TV, radio, and in newspapers. The swindlers may cloak themselves in the legitimacy of the IRS by promoting so-called IRA-approved investments (see chapter 5) or seek to evade consumer protection laws by claiming to represent unregulated general partnerships or limited liability companies.

These tips from the BBB, NASAA, and the FTC will help investors protect themselves from the fast-growing ranks of high-tech swindlers:

- *Be suspicious of any telemarketer who refuses to provide all representations in writing.* This is particularly true of profit projections or estimates of how much money you will have to invest before receiving a return on your investment. Scam artists often refuse to provide representations in writing because they do not want to leave behind evidence that they have falsified information.

- *Be skeptical of any unsolicited phone calls or e-mail messages about investments.* Think twice before buying investments from salespeople you do not know. Remember that an unsolicited call can be made from anywhere—even a jail.

- *Be suspicious of sales pitches that downplay risks or portray written risk disclosures as "routine formalities" required by the government.* No potential high-return investment is low-risk, no matter what telemarketers or promotional materials say. If risk disclosure statements tell you that you could lose your whole investment, believe them!

- *Do not be swayed by a smooth sales pitch or descriptions of high-technology riches.* Scammers spend years going from fraud to fraud, and all that experience makes them clever liars. They have an answer for everything, often because they use scripts with canned replies to a potential investor's every objection.

- *Be cautious of investment promotions comparing your potential investment to investments made by well-known businesses and individuals.* These investors generally achieved their gains by investing thousands or even millions of dollars developing communications businesses—not by giving their money to telemarketers.

- *Be wary of claims that you can apply for a license and let other companies buy, lease, and develop it.* In almost all cases, the FCC prohibits the acquisition of licenses for speculation or profitable resale. And in every case, the FCC requires the license holder to construct an appropriate communications system for the license, usually within one year. If this deadline is not met, the license expires and becomes worthless.

- *Beware of telemarketers who emphasize the "bells and whistles" of cutting-edge technology.* Remember that an undeveloped license provides *no* services without substantial capital investment and that many systems and licenses marketed to investors by phone do not actually provide any of the services that make the opportunity seem attractive.

- *Beware of promoters who say it is urgent to invest.* If investments are truly fast and furious, savvy entrepreneurs already will have snapped them up. Salespeople who call unknown investors over the phone are not likely to be pitching hot, high-quality investments.

- *Do not trust claims that well-known telecommunications companies will develop systems for your license or buy your license from you for a profit.* Before you invest, take the time to talk to representatives of these companies to gauge their interest.

- *Ask how much of the investment is going to "profit," "commissions," "broker's fees," "marketing costs," or similar items.* Application mills usually charge thousands of dollars for applications that cost hundreds. Fraudulent promoters of partnerships and limited liability companies leave consumers with little working capital and minimal assets. The more money going into sales expenses and costs, the greater the risk and the lower your return.

- *Do not be fooled by slick promotional materials, high-profile addresses, or toll-free numbers.* Remember that anyone can produce professional-looking literature, buy a toll-free number, or rent a mailbox at a prestigious address.

- *Demand proof for profit claims.* Legitimate telemarketers have a basis for their projections. Ask for reputable published data to back up all claims. Be wary of general statements that the industry is profitable and question all projections that are qualified as company opinion.

• *Determine how much money you will have to spend to obtain a return on your investment.* Keep in mind that developing advanced communications systems can cost millions of dollars. Fraudulent telemarketers who tell you that the cost of high technology is dropping may be describing rudimentary systems, not those capable of providing the advanced services being pitched.

• *Remember that the communications industry is highly competitive.* In most areas companies with substantial capital compete to provide communications services. As a license holder or shareholder in a partnership or company holding a license, you may have to compete with these big players to recover your investment.

• *Consult someone whose financial advice you trust, such as your banker, lawyer, accountant, or a financial planner with a solid reputation.* A registered securities broker also may provide insight about investing in high-tech industries. Your state securities agency (see Appendix B) can tell you whether the investment is lawfully registered with the state or is exempt from registration. Contact the FCC at 1-888-CALL-FCC (1-888-225-5322) to ask about the status of the license application process; applications may have been frozen or auctions for top markets may have been completed.

• *Check with your local Better Business Bureau (see Appendix A), state securities agency, or state attorney general to find out if complaints have been registered against the company that has approached you.* Keep in mind, though, that con artists often change names and locations and that new or renamed frauds may have no record of wrongdoing.

The FTC publishes a series of informative brochures on high-tech swindles, available by mail or through the Internet (see Appendix C). For information on how to report a suspected fraud and file a complaint, contact your state securities administrator or local Better Business Bureau.

Chapter 5

"IRA - Approved" Investment Schemes

After nearly forty years as a retail sales clerk, Mary was looking forward to retirement—to tossing out the alarm clock and at last having the free time to enjoy hobbies and travel. Since her divorce many years earlier, she had not been able to put away much in savings, but she had been conscientious about making yearly contributions to an Individual Retirement Account (IRA). Lacking knowledge and experience in investment alternatives, she had followed a friend's advice and placed her IRA funds in a mutual fund specializing in public utilities. Over the years this conservative investment had realized modest but consistent returns.

Flipping through the TV channels one evening, Mary came upon an interesting program. Speaking before an appreciative audience, an enthusiastic investment expert was explaining that millions of individuals who used their retirement funds merely to shelter income were missing out on a tremendous opportunity for equity growth. The more Mary listened to the expert's glowing descriptions of the kinds of profits available to wise investors, the more uncomfortable she became at the thought of the modest 6 to 7 percent returns she had been earning. When a toll-free number appeared on the screen, Mary grabbed a pencil. Her call was answered by a sympathetic operator who promised to rush her a packet of informative materials.

A few days later the literature arrived with a cover letter full of glowing promises. "Many of our current customers," the letter explained, "took substantial positions with us after comparing their actual IRA return of 3 to 5 percent to our 400 percent projected return. They simply did their homework, looked at all the facts, and decided that the investment was as safe as any around. It just happens to have a higher return!"

The letter was followed by a phone call from an investment respresentative. The details of the investment touted by the fast-talking caller were a little confusing—something to do with high-tech microwave technology and the wireless cable television industry—but the pitch was reassuring. After all, the caller said, Mary could roll over her IRA funds from the low-yield mutual fund account and place them in this much more profitable investment without paying any penalties or taxes. Certainly the opportunity must be solid, or the IRS would not allow such a transaction.

By the end of the call, Mary was convinced that this new investment was a quick path to easy street. The process of transferring her funds was easy. The necessary paperwork was included with the solicitation materials, and the friendly investment representative obligingly talked her through filling it out. Soon the documents were in the mail, and Mary looked forward to her first statement showing sky-high returns.

The statement, of course, never came. Mary's attempts to reach the investment promoter were useless. The toll-free number had been disconnected, and letters came back stamped "Box Closed." Phone calls and a letter to the television station that had aired the promoter's "infomercial" also hit a brick wall—the station disclaimed any responsibility for the accuracy of the ads it aired. In the end, Mary—along with an unknown number of other victims—lost 100 percent of her retirement nest egg.

A "New Generation"

Millions of individuals save for their later years with funds placed in IRAs, 401(K)s, Keogh plans, Simplified Employee Pension (SEP) plans, and 403(b) tax-sheltered annuities. These retirement savings vehicles allow investors to make yearly contributions that grow and compound tax-free until the funds are withdrawn. Under federal law, IRA dollars can be placed in almost any kind of investment, excluding a few categories such as art objects, antiques, stamps, and some other collectibles. However, most financial advisers urge investors to build their IRAs with a diversified balance of investments, which might include certificates of deposit, mutual funds, stocks, and taxable bonds.

In recent years there has been a major shift away from employer-controlled pensions toward IRAs and other self-directed retirement plans. That shift has placed billions of dollars of investment capital in the hands of a growing number of individual investors, including many who may be ill equipped to make informed investment decisions. Unscrupulous promoters of fraudulent investment schemes have been quick to take advantage of this opening.

At one time almost all illicit investment schemes were promoted through high-pressure telemarketing "cold calls." Promoters of this new generation of scams directed at IRA funds, however, use a different route to ply their illicit trade. So-called "IRA-approved" scams are often promoted through slick television infomercials (twenty- to thirty-minute TV advertisements) and radio ads. Viewers and listeners are invited to phone a toll-free number to get a package of materials, which is followed by a high-pressure phone sales pitch.

Self-Defense for Senior Investors

"IRA-approved" investment schemes are just one of the many ways con artists cheat senior citizens. In fact, senior investors —particularly women—are the investment con artist's number-one target. The following self-defense tips from the BBB and NASAA can help seniors avoid being victimized:

1. ***Do not be a "courtesy victim."*** Con artists often exploit the good manners of seniors who come from a generation that was taught always to be polite to phone callers and visitors. Remember that you are under no obligation to stay on the phone with a stranger who asks for your money. It is not impolite to simply explain that you are not interested and hang up the phone.

2. ***Check out strangers touting "strange" deals.*** A firm "no" is the best response to anyone who presses you to make an immediate decision regarding an investment before you have had an opportunity to check out the investment, the salesperson, and the firm. Be sure to get written information about all investments and to make sure you understand the risks involved. Also check with your state securities agency and the National Association of Securities Dealers (see Appendices B and C) for background information on investment salespeople and firms and on the proper registration of investment opportunities.

3. ***Always stay in charge of your money.*** Beware of financial professionals who offer to "handle everything," relieving you of the need to watch over your investment nest egg. Constant vigilance is a necessary part of being an informed investor. If you have little knowledge or experience in investing, take the time to educate yourself or seek the assistance of a trusted family member or a professional such as your banker or attorney.

4. ***Never judge integrity by how a person sounds.*** Con artists practice sounding professional, and they can make even the flimsiest investment deal sound safe. Some swindlers are extremely polite, knowing that many seniors are likely to equate good manners with personal integrity.

5. ***Watch out for salespeople who prey on your fears.*** It is common for swindlers to exploit a senior's anxieties about outliving their savings or seeing resources vanish in the wake of a costly illness or incapacity. Do not let fear cloud your judgment. An investment makes sense for you only when you can understand it and feel comfortable with the level of risk involved.

6. ***Exercise particular caution if you are a senior woman with little experience handling***

money. Many women now in their retirement years have received little or no training or education in how to handle money. As a result, senior women, particularly those receiving insurance payments as the result of the death of a spouse, are prime targets for con artists. Senior women who are on their own and unfamiliar with investment decision making should always seek the advice of a trusted family member or a disinterested professional, such as a banker or attorney, before deciding where to invest financial resources.

7. *Monitor your investments and ask tough questions.* Keep a close eye on the progress of your investment by insisting on regular written and oral reports. Be on the lookout for excessive or unauthorized trading of your funds, and do not be swayed by assurances that such practices are routine. If you suspect that something is wrong but are unable to get a satisfactory explanation, call your local Better Business Bureau or state securities agency to make a complaint.

8. *Be suspicious if you have trouble retrieving your principal or cashing out profits.* Unless you have invested in a vehicle with a fixed term, such as a certificate of deposit, you should be able to receive your funds or profits within a reasonable period of time. Alarm bells should sound if any individual with whom you have invested stalls when you ask for your principal, profits, or interest. Unscrupulous investment promoters not only pocket the initial investment funds of their victims, they often pressure investors to "roll over" nonexistent "profits" into new and even more alluring investments—thus further delaying the point at which their fraud will be discovered.

9. *Do not let embarrassment or fear keep you from reporting investment fraud or abuse.* Some senior investors who have been victimized in financial schemes hesitate to complain out of embarrassment or the fear that they will be considered incapable of handling their own affairs. Con artists often capitalize on those fears. Be aware that recognizing and reporting a scam early on increases the possibility of recovering some or all of your funds.

10. *Beware of "recovery" scams.* It is natural for a senior facing the loss of a lifetime of savings to panic. Con artists take advantage of that reaction with "recovery" schemes—promises to make good on losses and possibly even generate new returns. (For a further discussion of recovery schemes, see "A Second Bite" in chapter 9, "Boiler Rooms.")

By inducing likely victims to make the first call, the schemers make their work that much easier.

Promoters of "IRA-approved" schemes promise returns of 200 to 800 percent on tax-deferred retirement investments. Victims are lulled by the claim that the proposed investments are approved or otherwise endorsed by the Internal Revenue Service. The salesperson for one scam read from a pitch script that began, "I've been encouraged to call you by the IRS because you have some form of self-contributory, self-directed retirement program like an IRA." Another con artist assured an undercover securities investigator posing as a potential investor that his program was "IRA-sanctioned." Noting that there are no penalties for transferring funds from one IRA account to another, this salesperson concluded that "the government would not allow anything like that to happen if it was not something very solid for you to get into."

In reality, the IRS neither approves of specific IRA investments nor directly or indirectly advises retirement savers on what to do with their IRAs. Though IRA funds must be handled by a custodian such as a bank, trust department, or mutual fund, the custodian is not obligated to review or approve of the investments selected for self-directed IRAs.

A Selection of Schemes

State investment watchdog agencies estimate that tens of thousands of unwary consumers have invested hundreds of millions of dollars in bogus "IRA-approved" investment schemes that will prove largely or entirely worthless. The promoters of these schemes often peddle headline-grabbing new technologies such as wireless cable television, specialized mobile radio, and personal communication services (see chapter 4, "High-Tech Scams"). Touting investments in these new and largely untested technologies as a surefire path to instant riches, investment schemers exploit the inexperience of investors who are unaware of the enormous risks and uncertainties involved. Other "IRA-approved" schemes have involved investments in questionable real estate deals such as mortgage pools and in exotic livestock, including ostriches and emus.

These highlights from state securities agency files illustrate the diversity of "IRA-approved" investment schemes:

- The Indiana Division of Securities took action against a company that claimed it was raising money for the construction of a wireless cable television facility in southern Florida. The firm promised 500 percent in short-term profits for those who invested through IRAs. Claiming to have been involved in thirty to forty successful wireless cable TV projects, the company assured potential investors that the investment had little or no chance of failure. Investors also were told that the offering was a "general partnership" and thus was not required to register under federal and state securities laws. In fact, the firm held no licenses for wireless cable television in southern Florida and had no track record of success. Further, one of the firm's principals was already the subject of a Federal Trade Commission action for deceptive activities in an earlier cable TV scam.

- In a massive dragnet involving more than four hundred high-tech investment schemes, the California Department of Corporations discovered that investors had forked over a total of $12 million in retirement funds to the promoter of a bogus interactive video distribution service (IVDS) scheme. Investigators even discovered that the promoter was continuing to solicit investors from a telephone in a detention center. In another California case, investigators determined that just half of 1 percent of funds solicited from IRA savers for a wireless cable television project were actually going to the construction of the project.

- An ostrich farm investment scheme assured IRA savers that ostriches were the "agricultural industry of the century" and "the cash crop of the 1990s." Solicited to become "general partners" in the raising of $60,000 to maintain two breeder birds, IRA investors were lured with projected instant profits of 200 to 300 percent. Naturally the promoters made no mention of the extreme risks involved in the ostrich farming industry, including breeding difficulties, disease, and an uncertain commercial market. This scheme was the subject of regulatory action by several state securities agencies.

Outsmarting IRA Schemers

How can you avoid falling victim to an "IRA-approved" scheme? The key is to overlook slick sales pitches and tempting promises while exercising a healthy curiosity and skepticism. The following tips and precautions can help.

- *Be extremely cautious during the tax season when it comes to making IRA investments.* Just because the pressure is on to make a decision about your retirement plan contribution, do not make the mistake of going along with the first attractive sales pitch you hear. Also avoid making quick decisions on IRA investments if you are leaving a job and facing a sixty-day deadline for making a decision about where to roll over retirement savings or a pension profit-sharing plan.

- *Avoid any investment touted as approved or endorsed by the IRS.* This is a sure sign of fraud—the IRS does *not* endorse specific tax deals.

- *Take the time to check out additional sources of information regarding any investment you are considering.* Be cautious about investment ads broadcast on TV, particularly infomercials, or on the radio. Some investment-related radio talk show hosts receive payments for their personal endorsements of investment plans. You may want to check an infomercial's claims with the National Infomercial Marketing Association (NIMA) International (see Appendix C), whose members are required to adhere to generally accepted principles of ethical business conduct for producing and distributing infomercials.

- *Beware of promises of no-risk, sky-high returns on exotic investments.* High-tech investments may mean higher returns, but they also mean higher risks. An investment promising 200 or 300 percent returns in a short period of time with little or no risk *is* too good to be true.

• *Never transfer or roll over retirement funds directly to an investment promoter.* IRAs and other retirement funds must go to a pension fund administrator such as a bank, trust department, or mutual fund.

• *Proceed with caution when asked to invest in a "general partnership" or "limited liability company."* Many high-tech, real estate, and exotic livestock deals are packaged as unregulated "general partnerships" or "limited liability companies" so that fraudulent promoters can evade state and federal securities laws requiring the disclosure of key facts about themselves and their investment plans. However, in many instances, these deals are still securities, and therefore disclosure is required and should be made to prospective investors. Skirting the securities laws enables con artists to conceal personal bankruptcies, previous securities law violations, actual marketing costs, competing technologies, and other risk disclosures.

• *Do not be swayed by the fact that a bank or trust department is serving as an IRA custodian.* IRA custodians are not responsible for checking out the investments to which customers direct their funds.

• *Keep in mind that a "hot" industry does not necessarily translate into a hot company.* Promoters of illicit investment schemes may attempt to lend legitimacy to their claims by sending copies of articles from prominent business publications. Unless those articles specifically discuss the company that has approached you, they may not be relevant. Keep in mind that glowing news about an emerging high-tech industry does not mean that a specific company will be part of the overall success story.

• *Always check with your state securities agency to make certain an investment and its promoter are in compliance with securities laws and rules and with your local Better Business Bureau to determine the company's reliability.* Remember that even though written disclosure documents state that the deal is not subject to regulatory review as a security, it still might be.

Chapter 6

Investing Overseas

F ew North American investors have escaped the newspaper headlines, magazine articles, and television news reports touting the appeal of overseas investments. Hoping to tap into record gains in stocks, commodities, and other investment opportunities in foreign markets, a flood of consumers has been swept up in the global investing craze. Many brokers now follow time zones around the world, trading for their customers twenty-four hours a day.

Investing in global markets can be a legitimate means for diversifying investment portfolios and taking advantage of potential gains. However, consumers need to be aware of additional risks and considerations when investing overseas. There are major differences among national markets in procedures, practices, and rules. Some countries, for example, may have no prohibitions against insider trading and/or no government agency to safeguard the interests of investors and guard against marketplace misconduct. Here is how the prospectus for an international bond fund outlines the potential pitfalls of foreign investment:

> *These include risks relating to political or economic conditions in foreign countries, fluctuations in foreign currencies, withholding or other taxes, operational risks, increased regulatory burdens, and the potentially less stringent investor protection and disclosure standards of foreign markets. . . . All of these factors can make foreign investments, especially those in developing countries, more volatile than U.S. investments.*

Scams Go Global

Added to the risks involved in legitimate overseas investments are the perils posed by a new breed of con artists who have cashed in on the rush to global investing. Quick to pick up on the psychology of current investment trends, these scammers have gone international. Operators of high-pressure telemarketing boiler rooms have evaded North American law enforcement agencies by moving offshore, often to countries where bank secrecy laws make it virtually impossible to seize stolen assets. Other scammers have adopted foreign bases for the promotion of old-age pyramid schemes or up-to-the-minute scams on the Internet. Inventive international investment cons have touted precious metals, mining, penny stocks, coins, currency speculation, foreign lotteries, nonexistent foreign banking instruments, and even phony coconut plantations. Consumers ranging from small investors to sophisticated handlers of corporate pension funds have lost billions of dollars to these types of scams. Here's a look at some of the most prevalent overseas investment scams.

Prime Bank Guarantee Scams

Law enforcement officials have noted a recent increase in schemes involving the promotion of questionable financial instruments called prime bank guarantees. Other names for these instruments include prime bank notes, prime bank letters of credit, prime European bank letters of credit, prime world bank debentures, and prime insurance guarantees. Con artists promoting prime bank-type instruments claim to have access to a secret market in these instruments, which they say are securities guaranteed by a large, well-known foreign bank. Consumers are guaranteed returns as high as 2 percent a week—nearly 300 percent a year—on investments in prime bank guarantees. Some individual and institutional investors have been talked into pooling their funds to purchase the instruments. Others have paid advance loan fees to obtain loans supposedly funded in some manner by prime bank-type instruments. Con artists often use forged references and claim they have the backing of well-known foreign banks. When contacted by potential borrowers or investors, those institutions invariably have no knowledge about the unauthorized use of their names or the issuance of any type of prime bank financial instrument.

According to federal financial institution supervisory agencies, there is no apparent legitimate use of any prime bank-type instrument, and investors "should be alert to the potential dangers associated with any transaction involving these types of instruments." The Securities and Exchange Commission (SEC) further warns that "many of the illegal and dubious schemes . . . appear to involve overly complex loan funding mechanisms," a fact that, "in the eyes of an unsophisticated investor . . . may make a questionable investment appear worthwhile." Even sophisticated investors have lost significant sums to these types of scams. One U.S. investor who wired $100,000 to a swindler's account at a top British bank was told he had missed the deadline for joining the investment program. When he attempted to recover his funds, the luckless investor was warned that if he made trouble, the scammers would destroy his personal credit rating. The swindlers went so far as to threaten that he would "never get a checking account again."

Foreign Lottery Scams

According to the U.S. Postal Service, thousands of U.S. citizens have been bilked out of millions of dollars in foreign lottery scams. Typically a consumer receives a brochure in the mail offering convenient mail-order purchases of lottery tickets from a foreign country. Some offers involve the pooling of investors' funds to purchase tickets, with all participants receiving a share of the "winnings." In actuality, not only are there no winnings, but consumers who mail in their money never see a lottery ticket or any other evidence that tickets were bought. In some cases telemarketing scammers pushing foreign lottery swindles have talked consumers into investing via their credit cards. Once scammers have the card numbers, they make repeated unauthorized transactions on the accounts.

The Better Business Bureau in Vancouver, British Columbia reported being deluged with inquiries and complaints from U.S. consumers about two types of businesses: advance fee loan brokers and companies involved in the sale of offshore lottery tickets. According to the Bureau, the complaints regarding the sale of offshore lottery tickets alleged unauthorized, continuing credit card and checking account debits/transactions, misrepresentations involving winnings, high-pressure sales tactics over the telephone, and threats of collection when consumers stop playing the lotteries.

Consumers who receive a foreign lottery offer through the mail should be aware that sending lottery materials—including letters and circulars, tickets or papers claiming to represent lottery tickets, and payments to purchase tickets—is prohibited by U.S. federal law. Most foreign lottery solicitations sent by mail do not come from foreign government agencies or licensees but from overseas scammers operating without the knowledge or consent of any government agency.

Scams on the Internet

The rising popularity of on-line computing has given con artists a new means of perpetrating foreign investment frauds (also see chapter 10, "On-line Investment Fraud"). In one case promoters promised investors astronomical profits from a worldwide telephone lottery. The on-line offer promised that investors who paid $129 for membership in the plan could expect maximum returns of more than $10,000 per week for recruiting other investors via the Internet. SEC officials noted that the operation, which raised more than $3 million in less than a year, misrepresented and failed to disclose legal and technological restrictions on the proposed lottery. The promoters started a similar lottery in Germany after an SEC action shut them down in the United States.

International Telemarketing Fraud

Boiler-room operators have used the phone lines to promote foreign investment scams involving prime bank guarantees, foreign currency or bond markets, nonexistent mining operations, phony certificates of deposit and savings accounts in offshore banks in exotic locales, and more (also see chapter 9, "Boiler Rooms"). It can be difficult or impossible to investigate and prosecute fraudulent telemarketers in foreign countries. In most cases victims never recover their funds.

The Wisconsin securities administrator's office cautions investors against an increasingly common form of fraud, which has been advancing across the country from California and Vancouver for several years now. In this one, it is claimed that the sellers are connected with sophisticated traders in European bank notes or the like. The trading programs are frequently referred to as "rolls." Usually it is claimed that millions of dollars in trading profits can be made with only a few thousand dollars of investment. Sometimes the claim is made that the investors' funds will be used to purchase some sort of security bond for the program. The Wisconsin administrator's office has never seen one of these deals that has not turned out to be fraudulent. This is a classic illustration of the maxim that "If it sounds too good to be true, it probably is [too good to be true]." One common feature to date has been that when one asks detailed questions about how the program could actually work, the answers—if there are any—are pretty much unintelligible gobbledygook.

Pyramid Schemes

One international pyramid scheme spanned Ontario, British Columbia, and Europe. About 10,000 investors were conned out of $36 million by a foreigner who promised high returns on investments in a scheme known as the System B. Investors were told their money was being put into international currency and commodity markets. In reality the funds went into the promoter's pocket.

Unregistered and Falsely Represented Securities

Cases that have been investigated include the following:

- An unregistered foreign investment company sold unregistered securities throughout the United States. Promotional materials mailed by the company and its trustee solicited minimum investments of $200 to establish personal offshore trusts, the assets of which were to be pooled for investment in the firm. Profits from 100 to 280 percent were advertised. At least twelve state securities agencies have issued cease-and-desist orders against the company.

- An Ohio man was persuaded to invest $200,000 in a project to remove slag from Canada's Ottawa River. Two Ohio-based firms were involved in the transaction—American Floatation Technology (AFT), which promoted a technology involving the separation of precious metals, and Canadian Gold, which ostensibly was raising financing for a Canadian business that had a grant from the Canadian government to operate the dredging project. AFT's president promised the investor that his funds would be forwarded to the Canadian firm. In return the investor would receive a percentage of the returns from the minerals found in the materials extracted from the river. The truth was that neither of the Ohio companies had rights to participate in the slag removal project; they simply divided the investors' $200,000 between them. After an investigation, the Ohio Division of Securities presented AFT's president with a cease-and-desist order, delivered to the Ohio correctional facility where he was incarcerated.

Be Informed About International Investing

Enforcing actions against con artists operating beyond the reach of domestic law enforcement is extremely difficult and, in some cases, virtually impossible. Your best defense against international investment swindles, according to the BBB and NASAA, is to take some simple steps to protect your interests.

1. ***Do not be stampeded in the rush to international investing.*** Business news and fellow investors can easily give you the impression that *everyone* is investing overseas. Be cautious about letting current trends influence your decisions. Make sure your investment is appropriate for your financial objectives and ability to assume risk. Also be wary of on-line hyping of international investment opportunities through computer bulletin boards, chat rooms, and unsolicited e-mail messages. A flurry of on-line interest in a little-known stock can be a warning sign of a "pump and dump" scam (see chapter 10, "On-Line Investment Fraud").

2. ***Educate yourself about global markets.*** Before you can make informed investment choices, you will need to know something about practices in the foreign markets you are considering. Make sure you understand how investments are regulated and how investors are protected from investment and abuse. How would you go about resolving disputes related to your investment? Do you know what

government agencies would assist you in resolving problems?

3. ***Remember that international is not always better.*** Investing overseas may be "hot" today, but the quality of investment opportunities in other nations is not necessarily higher than those at home. In fact, because of enforcement complications, the level of risk in overseas investment may be considerably higher, even in mainstream market products. Further, once your money is gone, it may be impossible to recover.

Pawns of the Prince

What would you do if a Nigerian prince offered to transfer several million dollars into your business bank account? A number of U.S. business executives have jumped at the chance—and lost huge amounts of money.

Here is how the scam works: A company receives a letter from a mysterious Nigerian businessman with an impressive title such as "prince" or "chief." The letter explains that the writer, acting with the knowledge of the Nigerian government, is contacting the firm to request assistance in transferring a large sum of money, usually $10 million to $30 million, into the United States. The surplus funds, supposedly just discovered in a Nigerian government bank account, will be invested in U.S. goods and services. All the company receiving the letter needs to do is agree to act as a partner, allowing the Nigerian government to transfer the funds into the company's U.S. bank account. In return, the company will receive a fee of 30 percent or more of the amount transferred.

Executives who fall for the scam are asked to send signed blank sheets of company letterhead, the name and address of their bank, plus their bank account numbers, so the Nigerian officials can proceed with the funds transfer. Funds indeed are transferred—right out of the unwitting victims' accounts. In some cases executives have paid "taxes" prior to the expected transfer. One victim paid out more than $400,000 before reporting the fraud. In other cases U.S. executives who traveled to Nigeria to meet their partners were asked to put down "deposits" to show good faith and defray their hosts' expenses. One visitor was forced to turn over $4,000 in travelers' checks before he was allowed to leave the country.

4. *Keep in mind that trouble often follows when you deal with a stranger about something you cannot check out personally.* Do not be deceived by slick brochures that make an enterprise look legitimate. The fact that persuasive promoters say they have an oil well in Europe or a gold mine in South Africa does not mean you have enough information to make an investment decision. In general, investors are best advised to deal with people they know and in investments they understand. Think hard before

In one bizarre twist this scam claimed as its victim an Idaho con artist whose specialty was the sale of unregistered securities in various fraudulent schemes involving vending machines. In order to raise capital, ostensibly for a video game business, the man advertised for investors. One respondent to his ads was a California resident who claimed to have purchased an oil contract involving Nigeria and China that obligated the Nigerian government to pay him $25.5 million. The California man offered the Idaho con artist $5 million if he would assist in obtaining certain fees required by the Nigerian government. The Idaho man agreed and engaged in a variety of scams to raise the funds, including investment schemes targeted at other respondents to his video game ads. He was eventually convicted of securities fraud and loan fee fraud after an investigation by the Idaho Securities Bureau.

As implausible as the Nigerian prince scam sounds, U.S. Postal Inspectors report that it has defrauded many unwary investors. This old-fashioned confidence swindle has been around for years and snags hundreds of victims each year.

According to one local Better Business Bureau official, "This is one of those around-the-world things that never stops. It just changes form." Another Better Business Bureau reported that the 250 Nigerian letters in its files had thirty different signatures on them and of those, fourteen had the same telephone number. They were just signing different names."

One investor located in the Bureau's service area had sent an $1,800 check to Nigeria and was two days away from boarding a plane to the country when he saw a television report on the scam. Another investor, according to the Bureau, paid so heavily into the scheme —over $20,000—that she refused to believe authorities when first warned it was a scam.

giving up your money if you do not have the contacts or financial resources to personally inspect an investment.

5. *You can invest in individual foreign securities through U.S. brokers or mutual funds.* Many foreign securities are traded on U.S. exchanges in the form of American Depository Receipts (ADRs). These are subject to SEC and exchange regulations. Many

The Bre-X Gold Scam

The president of the Toronto Stock Exchange called it a "comet" (a once-in-a-lifetime scam so stupendous that "all the disclosure rules in the world will not protect either the gullible investor or, it seems, even the most sophisticated one." From 1996 to 1997, individual and institutional investors, including mutual fund companies and pension plans, snapped up millions of shares of stock in an Alberta-based mining firm, Bre-X Minerals Ltd. Sold initially through private placements, Bre-X's stock later was listed on Canadian and U.S. stock exchanges. Its price climbed from an initial private offering price at 30 cents a share to more than $250 on the open market with both market-wise investors and less-experienced individuals joining the stampede. The basis for the boom: Bre-X's claim that it had discovered the world's largest gold deposit in the jungles of Indonesia.

To outsiders—including top U.S. and Canadian brokerage firms and a respected independent engineering firm—those claims looked legitimate. But two years after Bre-X's first optimistic statements, the scheme began to unravel when independent drilling programs at the site found no gold. Investigations revealed that Bre-X had doctored samples of rock drawn from the site, "salting" the worthless rocks with gold dust en route to the testing lab. One of the miners who uncovered the scheme called it a tampering operation "without precedent in the history of mining anywhere in the world."

Today Bre-X's stock is worthless. Criminal investigations are underway in Canada and Indonesia. And investors who are tempted to bet their savings on the next pot of gold have yet another cautionary tale to consider.

international mutual funds are "dollar denominated," or U.S.-currency based, thus eliminating the risks of foreign currency fluctuations. For information on these, ask your broker and read the mutual fund prospectus.

6. ***Be cautious about prime bank guarantees.*** If you receive an investment offer based on a prime bank guarantee or similar financial instrument, contact your state securities regulators and the SEC.

7. ***Steer clear of foreign lottery solicitations.*** If you receive a foreign lottery solicitation through the mail, contact your local Better Business Bureau, and turn over the mailing to your local postmaster or nearest postal inspector.

8. ***Before making any investment, check out the promoter with your state securities agency.*** Claims that overseas investment promoters are exempt from state and federal securities law registration requirements are false and should raise a warning flag. Also check with your local Better Business Bureau and state attorney general's office for the promoter's record of consumer complaints and government actions.

Chapter 7

Vacation Time-Sharing

The term "time-share" was borrowed from the computer industry, which coined it to describe a plan whereby many individuals from remote locations could gain simultaneous access to a central computer bank. In real estate the term refers to the joint ownership or rental of a vacation property by a number of persons, with each occupying the property for short periods of time on an annual rotating basis. Participants can purchase one or two weeks of residence in a resort area at a cost far lower than that of year-round ownership.

Time-sharing has been a boon to thousands of individuals and families who have invested their money in resorts established and operated by responsible developers. The case of Jeremiah and Anne is a good example. Having vacationed happily in Bermuda for twenty years, the couple was becoming increasingly dismayed at the escalating hotel costs. It looked for a while as though they might have to take their vacations elsewhere. Then, on the recommendation of a friend, they visited a resort on St. George's Island that was in the process of converting to a time-share plan.

Jeremiah and Anne knew the resort as a cluster of white cottages in the oldest section of Bermuda. They had always loved St. George's, known for its crooked streets, its tiny alleyways with names like Petticoat Lane, Featherbed Alley, and Turkey Hill, and its ancient forts and lighthouses. They were almost reluctant to visit, fearing that this elegant historic section of Bermuda would be even more expensive than the others. But time-sharing proved to be the answer to their dilemma, prompting them to make one of the best investments of their lives. For the sum of $8,100, they were guaranteed one week's occupancy each year for a period of twenty-five years in a handsomely appointed and furnished two-bedroom house.

Examples similar to Jeremiah and Anne's can be cited in multitudes of choice locations from Florida and the Carolinas to the White Mountains of New Hampshire, and from the sun-drenched shores of California and Hawaii to quite a few locations abroad. But for every glorious case history on record, there is at least one that is tinged with problems ranging all the way from outright fraud and deception to mismanagement and lack of foresight.

The Flip Side

George and Susan had worked hard during twenty-five years of marriage to acquire an attractive home and put their three children through school and college. Although vacations, sometimes in the form of motor trips and sometimes at a rented cottage by a lake or at the seashore, had always been pleasant, the one thing they longed for was a second home in a permanent location. The dream had always eluded them because of tuition, taxes, and other expenses that took priority—that is, until they heard about the time-shares that were becoming available in a resort community in their favorite vacation destination, Vermont.

Familiarizing themselves with the time-share program, George and Susan began to wonder why they had never taken advantage of this alluring opportunity before. In essence it seemed quite simple: A relatively modest investment would buy them a piece of one of the resort condominiums being built for occupancy the following year. They and the other co-owners would take turns using the property, which was adjacent to areas offering swimming, sailing, golf, tennis, skiing, and other forms of recreation. The best part was that they would be established in a community that they could return to and be a part of each year, rather than taking their chances with whatever places were available at affordable rates.

George and Susan purchased their Vermont time-share and began looking forward to the following winter, when the whole family would enjoy two weeks of skiing. In the meantime, they would have the pleasure of looking over the architect's plans and keeping abreast of the progress of construction.

The first hint of trouble came in a memorandum indicating a "delay in the timetable." The wording was vague but hinted that the promoters had decided to hold up on one stage of construction until they could obtain "certain hardwoods of the durability we are demanding for this top-quality facility." Other indications of trouble followed in rapid succession, the most frustrating being the inability to contact the promoters or their salespeople by phone or mail. Finally, in desperation, George and Susan hired an attorney and demanded the return of their investment. But by then it was already too late. The promoters had filed for bankruptcy, and the couple would be lucky to get back fifty cents on the dollar.

It turned out that the real estate developer had started with good intentions but a total lack of experience with anything other than the construction of tract houses. Relying on poor financial counsel, the developer did not foresee the costs that would eventually cause the venture's downfall.

Pleasures and Perils

Time-sharing is a $5 billion industry worldwide. Over three million families participate in time-sharing each year, enjoying resorts that otherwise might not have been economically available to them. Across the country and around the world, time-shares have been sold in condominiums, apartments, single-family dwellings, campgrounds, and even recreational vehicles, yachts, cruise ships, and houseboats.

In a typical time-sharing program, a residential unit at a ski resort, beach condominium, mountain lodge, or similar vacation retreat is made available for a specific segment of time (usually one or two weeks) annually. Time-share prices vary greatly, depending on the quality of the accommodations and related facilities, the location, and the season (for example, a winter week in a warm climate costs more than a summer week in the same spot). In 1995 asking prices for a week in a studio unit averaged about $6,700; for a three-bedroom condominium, about $13,400.

Generally, time-share investors make a down payment and pay the rest of the purchase price in installments, with the sale financed by the developer or an outside source. Most buyers also pay annual maintenance fees and a fee for membership in an exchange program, which offers them the opportunity to trade the use of their resort unit for a week or two in another unit in a different location.

There are two basic types of time-share plans—"fee-simple" (also known as "deeded" agreements) and "right-to-use" (also known as "nondeeded" or "lease" agreements). A fee-simple time-share gives an investor an ownership interest in a residential unit. In essence, this is the same as getting together with a group of friends and buying a vacation home that will be used by all, in an agreed-upon rotation. The co-owners of the time-share are provided with a deed and have the right to sell or rent their share of the property within whatever restrictions have been predetermined by the developer. All co-owners are automatically members of an owner's association, which assumes control of the resort from the developer once most of the units and available time segments have been sold. In many cases the owner's association will

Time-Share Resale Schemes

If you own a vacation time-share and are approached by someone offering to help you find a buyer, be cautious. Some time-share resale programs are con games. Here is how they work: A bogus resale company phones you or sends a postcard asking you to call a particular number. The enthusiastic salesperson at the other end of the line assures you that the market for time-share resales is hot, with buyers snapping up units like yours for prices equal to or greater than the original purchase price. How can you contact the company's extensive list of sales agents and eager buyers? Simply by sending an advance listing fee, often around $300 to $500. The salesperson may even offer you a money-back guarantee or a $1,000 government bond if your time-share is not sold within the year.

The only real guarantee, if you are unwise enough to turn your money over to a strange voice on the phone, is that your name will join the names of other victims on the con artist's "sucker list." In reality, the market for time-share resales is generally poor, and the scammer's list of sales agents and buyers is likely to consist of people who have never heard of the company or have no interest in buying a time-share. It is doubtful that the company can sell your time-share at all, let alone at a profit. Many consumers whose time-shares are not resold within a year never recover their fee; some are presented with a bond worth as little as $60 or $70.

One South Florida Better Business Bureau tracked several bogus "Listing" services that required upfront fees but did not actively market the time-share properties; the BBB advised consumers who wanted to sell a time-share to call a real estate agent in the town where the unit is located and get a realistic appraisal.

Before turning over any money to a company offering to help you resell a time-share, ask for written materials on the company and its offer. Also ask for references, including the names and telephone numbers of consumers who have used the company's services. Check these references, and also check out the company with calls to your local Better Business Bureau, state attorney general's office, and state real estate licensing board. Finally, be cautious about any resale company charging an advance listing fee. Consider opting instead for a firm that agrees to collect its fee after your time-share is sold.

elect to retain the developer to manage the property, although it has the option of hiring an outside management firm.

A right-to-use time-share agreement entitles the buyer to use a residential unit for specified periods of time for a specified number of years, which may be as few as five years or as many as forty years. This type of plan is similar to buying a membership in a club or resort community. Buyers do not hold title to any property, and there may be limits on their resale rights.

Fee-simple units are usually more expensive than right-to-use units, but they may provide some tax benefits and they allow the buyer to have a voice in the management of the resort. Also, because investors in right-to-use time-shares do not actually own any portion of the property, their entire investment may be lost if the time-share project fails. However, some states have passed laws making reimbursement funds available to cover at least part of the loss. Also, some states require registration, the issuance of a prospectus by promoters, and/or a cooling-off period after sales, during which buyers can rescind their purchase without penalty. If the time-share is being offered with an emphasis on its investment potential, the seller may be required to register with state securities agencies. Check with your state securities administrator for information on state laws and regulations affecting time-share transactions.

One of the most auspicious developments in time-sharing has been the entry of large corporations into the industry. Their participation makes it more likely that investors will at least get their money back if a time-share venture fails or if the investors believe they have been misled by the developer's advertising and promotion. Large corporations also typically have the backup funds and clout necessary to obtain the choice sites that investors expect for their money, as well as the experience to realistically estimate maintenance and improvement costs. Equally important, reliable developers generally are able to establish realistic timetables, so that investors can determine the availability of time-share units for the dates and locations desired.

Unfortunately, even the involvement of large corporations and increasingly tough state regulations have not altogether shut the door on the "quick-buck" artists who exploit the popularity of time-sharing. Clever con artists usually can find a way to get around regulations. For example, hundreds of investors were attracted to a renovated Florida beachfront motel after visiting a handsome model studio-and-kitchen unit. Arriving for their week's vacation, these time-share owners were dismayed to find themselves assigned to a damp, depressing room that had not seen a fresh coat of paint in years. When they complained to state officials, investigators discovered that the developer had not set up an escrow account, as Florida law required, to hold the purchasers' down payments. It turned out that the promoter was already facing criminal charges in another state for having perpetrated a similar time-share fraud.

Ten Tips for Time-Sharers

Time-sharing can allow you to realize your vacation dreams . . . or it can become a nightmare in which the promoter's promises go unfulfilled and your investment dollars go down the drain. Before signing any agreements or paying any fees, you will want a clear understanding of what you are buying and from whom. The following precautions can help you evaluate the potentials and pitfalls in a time-share investment and ensure that your dreams do not fall victim to poor planning, mismanagement, or fraud.

1. Do not look at a time-share strictly as a real estate investment opportunity. The future value of a time-share depends on many unpredictable factors, and resale may be difficult. It is more realistic to think of a time-share as a prepaid vacation plan and to consider its costs as an expenditure, just like an annual vacation.

2. Plan to visit the site before you invest, to check out the residential units, the recreational facilities, and the surrounding area. Make certain the place is one you will want to return to year after year.

Real Estate Limited Partnerships

In the 1980s millions of U.S. investors poured an estimated $45 billion into real estate limited partnership (LP) investment programs. Like other forms of limited partnerships, real estate LPs are legal entities consisting of one or more general partners, who provide management for the underlying business, and limited partners, who pitch in the capital for business operations. Funds of LP investors have gone into the construction of new commercial office space, shopping malls, subsidized housing, and other projects.

For a time real estate LPs looked like an investor's dream come true, offering an opportunity to cash in on rising property values and generate enormous tax write-offs. Then the bubble burst, as the national real estate market took a downturn and dramatic tax law changes eliminated most tax shelter write-offs. Forced to stand on their own merits as investments, an estimated one in five LP deals foundered, taking investors'

dollars with them.

On top of honestly incurred losses, many investors in real estate limited partnerships found themselves the victims of fraud and misrepresentation. Complaints against partnership promoters detailed numerous cases in which brokerage firms and financial planners, motivated by the prospect of earning large commissions, sold real estate syndication deals to unsophisticated investors through the use of high-pressure sales tactics. In one group of eight LP deals involving energy-generating windmill farms in California, the Internal Revenue Service ruled that offering documents overstated the value of the windmills by 288 percent.

Some embittered investors in real estate LPs have sought to bail out of their partnerships by reselling their interests. A number of brokerage firms have become major players in the LP secondary market. Some of these match up buyers and sellers, while others are bargain hunters looking to scoop up partnership interests for their own accounts and then resell them. Questions have been raised about the sales practices of some secondary market trading firms, which in some cases have charged excessive markups and commissions.

If you are seeking to sell your interest in a real estate LP, the following tips can help you navigate the tricky waters of the resale market:

- Get your facts straight. Learn everything you can about your investment so that you can do the best job of selling it. Ask the promoter for the latest financial statements and current net asset value per unit as well as for any projection of future values. Determine whether the sponsor of the LP deal has any interest in repurchasing the units. Sometimes prices obtained from sponsors are better than those found elsewhere. Also consider going back to the broker or financial adviser who sold you the investment to see if that individual has other clients who are in the market.

- Negotiate to get the best price. Get several bids, then go back to your highest bidders, tell them what your top offer is, and ask if they can do better.

- Remember that the price you get may not be firm. Unlike a stock traded on an exchange, an LP has no established secondary market price. Resale brokers quoting you a price may simply be indicating what they think is possible.

- Understand the motivation behind the broker's price. Ask if the broker is acting as an agent (who will match you up with a buyer) or as a principal (who is buying for the brokerage firm's own account). Agents will tell you what they think might be a possible price, while principals will tell you how much their firm is willing to pay— an amount that may be negotiable.

- Ask about the settlement time. It can take from five business days to as long as two months to get paid for LP interests that have been sold.

- Find out about fees and commissions. Insist that your broker provide you with details about what you would pay in any potential transaction.

3. If the time-share's exchange program is an important part of your buying decision, investigate the limits on exchange opportunities. There usually is no guarantee that you will be able to trade use of your unit for accommodations at the location and time you prefer. Remember, too, that exchange programs rate units according to desirability. If you buy into a project that is not highly rated, you probably will not be able to "trade up" to a larger unit, a more appealing location, or a more desirable time of year. Also, unless you are certain of the exact time of the year that you want to use the unit, find out whether there is a realistic plan for swapping dates of occupancy with other investors.

4. Be wary of salespeople who use high-pressure tactics or urge you to invest quickly before the units are sold out. Also do not be swayed by the use of promotions such as "free" vacation certificates, gifts, or prizes as inducements to attend a sales presentation. Common promotional giveaways include gems with little or no material value, "gold" ingots with little gold content, and vacation awards that do not cover major costs such as food and travel.

5. Before signing any documents, make sure you understand every detail regarding your participation, rights, and options. Consider seeking outside professional counsel to advise you. Also make sure everything the salesperson promised verbally is written into the contract.

6. Consider all the costs involved in the time-share purchase, including mortgage payments, annual maintenance and exchange fees, and travel expenses to and from the vacation site. Make sure the contract spells out maintenance requirements and ask whether there are any limits on the rate at which maintenance fees can rise. Check with a local real estate agent to compare the total cost of the time-share with rental rates for similar accommodations in the same location.

7. If you are purchasing a deeded time-share, it is important to know

when your title will become free of any claims by the financial institution holding the property's mortgage. Usually that does not occur until a large percentage of time segments have been sold in your particular unit and you have paid the developer in full. Also look for a nonperformance clause in your contract. This clause should allow you to keep all your ownership rights even if a third party such as a bank is required to buy out your contract.

8. If you are buying a right-to-use time-share, look for what is called a nondisturbance provision. This ensures that you will continue to have the use of your time-share unit even if the developer or management firm defaults. The clause must not only be in your agreement with the developer but also in the mortgage or construction loan agreement granted to the developer by the financial institution involved.

9. If you are considering purchase of a time-share on property where the facilities have not been completed, ask for a written commitment from the sellers that the facilities will be finished as promised. Be aware that, in some cases, buyers have lost their investments when their money went into construction costs of a time-share that failed. Requiring that your down payment be held in escrow may provide some protection if the developer defaults.

10. Check out the track record of the time-share's seller, developer, and management company through your local Better Business Bureau (see Appendix A). Ask the seller for a copy of the current maintenance budget and look into the long-term plans for managing and repairing the property, replacing furnishings as needed, and providing promised services. Also make sure the project is registered with the real estate commission in the state where the property is located and that it is registered for sale in your state. If the time-share is being sold as an investment, state law may require that it be registered with regulating agencies; for information contact your state securities agency (see Appendix B).

Chapter 8

Ponzis and Pyramids

Mr. Johnson was a pleasant young man with a background in insurance, finance, and real estate. A Nevada resident, Johnson was attracted to the opportunities offered by the state's rapid growth in both residential and commercial real estate. For several years Nevada had been on a rocketship ride, with an influx of new residents at the rate of 5,000 per month to the Las Vegas area alone. Thanks to this robust growth, licensed mortgage brokers were offering 12 to 13 percent returns on investments in mortgages, or trust deeds, as they are called in Nevada. With his real estate background, Johnson decided to cash in on the financial opportunities of selling trust deeds to investors.

A mailing to prospective investors promised returns of 16 to 18 percent on investments in trust deeds. These high rates of return were possible, Johnson told prospects, because their funds would be invested in trust deeds secured by property that he himself owned. The smooth-talking young man chose his targets carefully. He sought out senior individuals with high net worth who were looking for returns higher than current market rates and who had previously invested in trust deeds. Polished and professional, Johnson was adept at disarming these potential investors and deflecting their questions. Victims later described him as the "nicest young man who always dressed so professionally."

Johnson managed to solicit funds totaling nearly $500,000 before any investors became suspicious. He kept his operation going by employing the tactics of a typical Ponzi scheme. Early investors were paid high returns out of monies solicited from new investors. Delighted with their good fortune, paid-off investors usually invested more money in other trust deeds. It took nearly a year and a half for Johnson's scam to reach the stage where there was no longer enough "fresh money" from new investors to pay earlier investors their returns.

When this Ponzi scheme finally unraveled, state securities division investigators discovered that Johnson had never owned most of the properties on which he was selling trust deed investments. The few properties that he did own were severely encumbered with liens and judgments that put investors in the fifth, sixth, or even tenth position to the first trust deed instead of the second position, as Johnson claimed. Investigators also found that Johnson's licenses with the state insurance and real estate divisions had been revoked and that several prior civil judgments had been filed against him. In all, investors lost a total of more than $450,000, money that this personable young con artist had used to support a lavish lifestyle. The Nevada Securities issued a Permanent Cease and Desist Order against Johnson and his business entities barring them from offering and selling the trust deed investments.

Charles Ponzi's Plan

Ponzi schemes take many forms, but the distinguishing feature of this type of operation is paying off early "investors" with money coming in from new victims. A Ponzi scheme may operate for some time before the promoter "pulls the plug"—that is, either disappears with all the investments or reveals the bad news that investments have gone "sour." A major factor in the eventual collapse of these schemes is the fact that there is no significant source of income other than that derived by roping in new investors.

The principal swindlers in many Ponzi schemes attract their prospective victims by radiating an aura of confidence and the assurance of wanting to share the wealth. In some cases the promoters even believe that their investment schemes will work, as though they have discovered some kind of magic formula overlooked by professional financiers. Then, when they realize there are hitches but that they could profit enormously by using other people's money, they invent a company and make all kinds of exorbitant claims.

Such was the case with Charles Ponzi, from whom the name of the swindle is derived. An Italian immigrant who moved to Boston in 1919, Ponzi learned that he could make a small profit by buying International Postal Reply Coupons (IPRCs), which could be redeemed for stamps in a number of countries. If he bought the stamps at a low rate in a weak-currency country such as Spain and then redeemed them at a higher price in the United States, he could make a profit on the widely varying rates of exchange.

Greed quickly overran Ponzi's modest intentions. He began to solicit investments from other people with the promise that, at a time when typical interest rates were only about 5 percent, his investment would produce a 40 percent return in just three months. The plan might have worked had there been enough IPRCs in circulation to support large-scale purchases. But the coupons were distributed in very limited quantities, expressly for the convenience of postal customers who used international mails. By the time interest in the scheme had escalated and Ponzi saw orders flooding in, he had become obsessed with the idea of making huge amounts of money. By giving some investors the 40 percent returns promised—using the money of new participants to pay off earlier ones—he baited the trap, and he was not averse to promising new investors 50 and eventually 100 percent returns in ninety days.

Even after Boston newspapers and law enforcement officials exposed the nature of Ponzi's swindle, money continued to pour into his office from victims who remained convinced that he had a good thing going and that they, too, could profit from his ingenuity. Many of those who lost heavily later blamed Massachusetts authorities for "butting in" and "victimizing" Charles Ponzi.

Although the Ponzi caper fleeced uncounted numbers of Bostonians out of a total of $10 million, the records revealed that this con artist had actually purchased less than $50 worth of International Postal Reply Coupons, most of them at the very start of the operation.

A New Lease on Lies

One of the startling facts about the Ponzi scam is that, although it has been around for nearly eighty years in one form or another and is one of the easiest swindles for regulators to detect, it is still prevalent today. The driving force behind the continuance of the Ponzi has been the introduction of new technologies and the many often bewildering new investments available to the public. In this crowded and fast-changing marketplace, Ponzi promoters have an increasing number of "costumes" at their disposal with which to dress up their schemes and shield them from ready detection.

In a sense investors themselves, through their eagerness to leap into a get-rich-quick plan, are to blame for the prevalence of Ponzi swindles, which always promise quick and massive profits. A few daring souls have even been known to invest deliberately in what they have spotted as a budding Ponzi scheme, convinced that they could anticipate the course of action and, at the right moment, take their money and run. Besides being morally and legally questionable, this type of reckless scheme is hardly recommended for the sensible investor.

Variations on the Ponzi scheme are numerous. In Utah, for example, the organist at a mortuary came up with the idea of soliciting the bereaved widows who were his boss's clients. By offering them high returns on what turned out to be nonexistent bonds in a fictitious finance company, the man bilked his victims out of $16.5 million before he was caught. In New Jersey, a food broker promised returns of 42 percent a year on investments in contracts to buy meat or poultry for resale to food distributors and retailers. Instead of going toward food purchases, the investors' money was used to finance such items as the promoter's $500,000 yearly salary and lavish lifestyle, which included frequent gambling trips to Atlantic City. In Alabama, a con artist made a mint in a bogus plan that involved the resale of designer jeans. A Texas woman took $17 million from investors in a phony chain of silver-recycling plants. And in Maryland, a promoter collected some $4 million from Baltimore-area residents by fraudulently promising them huge returns on largely nonexistent investments in diamonds and secondary mortgages.

The Ohio Division of Securities investigated a Ponzi scheme that involved the sale of unused cable television and low-power television air time. Investors were told they could double their money in sixty days because the air time would be resold at higher prices to people marketing unique gadgets they wanted to advertise on television. Some investors did get double their money back, however, they were encouraged to reinvest their money. These funds returned to some investors were really new investors' funds and not profits from air time sold, since only a small amount of air time was even purchased by the company.

The promoter was sentenced to 37–47 years of imprisonment after he was convicted by a jury on 117 counts of securities fraud, passing bad checks, perjury, and theft following a month-long trial in Wooster, Ohio.

Other swindles have involved just about any kind of deal you might imagine from gold mines and synthetic rubies to rock concert tickets, hydroponic farming, windmills, tropical islands, and adaptations of equipment used in outer space. But the alleged bottom line for prospective investors is always the same: the promise, indeed the *guarantee,* that they will receive investment returns far higher than the going rates.

Promoters also rely heavily on what has been described as the herd instinct. The start-up of a scam may be slow with a trickle of investors who take the bait. But once the plan builds momentum, word of mouth speeds it into high gear. For this reason swindlers focus their initial efforts with demography in mind. They may aim at people in the entertainment world, for example, knowing that news of a few successful participants will spread rapidly to others in the profession. In other cases momentum has been generated by concentrating on large church congregations, professional football players, government offices, city fire and police departments, and, of all things, an attorney's association.

The same focus is effective when applied regionally, concentrating initial activities at, say, an Air Force base, a single New England town, or a wealthy resort or retirement community. The early participants unwittingly aid and abet the swindler by passing along so-called confidential information that financial gains can be made by those in the know.

Often the initial participants in a Ponzi scam are rewarded with handsome returns on their investment, sometimes at interest rates that are astonishingly higher than the promoters originally promised. However, many of these people are so elated with their success that they turn right around and reinvest their money in the same ventures, often losing almost everything in the end. As one investor in a Ponzi scheme said sadly, "They would call me every week and tell me how many thousands of dollars I had made the week before and I'd write the figures down in my notebook. They looked so good on notebook paper. I should have written them down on toilet paper."

Be Informed About Ponzis

Here are basic rules to follow, offered by the BBB and NASAA, to avoid getting cheated by the Ponzi operators of the financial netherworld.

1. Ignore promises of high, guaranteed profits, the trademark of the Ponzi scam. Legitimate investment plans not only address themselves conservatively to any discussion of profits but rigorously avoid any promise of specific percentages over any given period.

2. Avoid any kind of investment that is not described clearly, in detail, and without hedging. Swindlers often declare that the specifics are "too technical" to describe in layperson's language. They may also avoid mentioning names on the grounds that the geniuses behind the plan "wish to remain anonymous."

3. Check out the promoter's credentials and background carefully through reliable sources that can alert you to any illegal acts or questionable practices.

4. Obtain information about the promoter and the proposed offering from your state securities agency and local Better Business Bureau. If you detect any violations of the law or securities registration, report your suspicions to these organizations or other appropriate agencies.

5. Demand detailed information *in writing.* Not only are you well within your rights to ask for documentation, but you will have every right to be concerned if the promoter is reluctant or hedges by asserting that such data is "confidential" or "classified."

6. Verify the claims and promises made by the promoter. Swindlers often try to imply that an offering is registered with a government agency or has the stamp of approval of a particular trust company. Victims too often accept such claims at face value and fail to verify the assertions.

7. Ask to visit the promoter's office or tour the plant where the "fabulous new product" is being manufactured. Suspicion should quickly set in if you are told that the office is being "renovated" or the plant is "under

tight security" and hence is off-limits to everyone except employees.

8. Back away from plans that offer "deferred" payments, where you have to invest today but will not see any products or evidence of ownership until the future. If, after investing, you are pressured into reinvesting or letting your profits "roll over," investigate at once.

9. Be on the alert for any kind of unbusinesslike conduct on the part of promoters, including an inability to reach them through phone calls or by mail. The farther along the route to disaster a Ponzi plan goes, the more impossible it becomes for victims to obtain information or get through to the promoters.

From Ponzis to Pyramids

Closely related to the Ponzi plan is the pyramid scheme. Sometimes the two go hand in hand, yet there is a distinction. The classic Ponzi amounts to little more than robbing an army of Peters to pay a handful of Pauls. As the number of investors grows and the supply of new investors dwindles, the Ponzi bubble bursts under the pressure of meeting promised payments. While some initial payments are actually made in order to drum up new recruits, the vast majority of investors in a Ponzi scheme end up losing all or most of their money.

By comparison, a pyramid scheme is a plan in which people invest in the right to sell the investment. Participants make money by enlisting new investors, who pay an initial fee for the right to sell the program to participants lower down the chain. Many pyramids attempt to establish their legitimacy by disguising themselves as multilevel marketing businesses.

In legitimate multilevel marketing, participants sign on as independent distributors, selling consumer products or services, usually in their own home or in customers' homes. Distributors also earn a percentage of the sales made by their downline sales force—the distributors they have personally recruited and trained to sell the products or services.

In a pyramid scheme, however, the product or service to be sold is largely ignored. Instead the focus is on the quick profits to be earned by recruiting others to invest, who in turn recruit others. The scheme inevitably collapses as participants keep recruiting new investors from the ever-decreasing number of prospects in a given area. The chart below, provided by the Securities and Exchange Commission, assumes that each investor in the pyramid scheme recruits six new participants and gives an example of how the number of investors needed to keep the scheme working can quickly exceed the population of the United States.

Month	Participants
1	6
2	36
3	216
4	1,296
5	7,776
6	46,656
7	279,936
8	1,679,616
9	10,077,696
10	60,466,176
11	362,797,056 (exceeding U.S. Population)

This chart also shows why these schemes are called pyramids—the promoters sit at the top of a pyramid-shaped flow of money. Money coming from later investors flows up toward the top. Being at the top may result in your receiving a lot of money quickly but, when approached with this type of offer, it is virtually impossible to determine just where you stand in the pyramid.

To join a pyramid, you might have to pay anywhere from a small investment to thousands of dollars. In some cases your investment may go to the purchase of nearly worthless products, if any products are involved at all. Often promoters build their scams on products that are cheap to produce but have no established market value, for example, an exotic cure or a new fungus culture ostensibly used in cosmetics manufacturing. It can be nearly impossible for prospects to gauge whether there is a real consumer market for these products.

While some participants in pyramid schemes invest with the knowledge that they are taking a gamble, many victims are fooled into believing that they are paying for assistance in starting a legitimate small business. Pyramid promoters are masters of group psychology. At recruiting meetings they know how to create an enthusiastic, frenzied atmosphere in which group pressure and promises of easy money play on people's greed and fear of missing out on a good deal. Pyramid schemes often exploit people with limited means and a limited knowledge of business. But the promise of a shortcut to riches can tempt even sophisticated investors.

Local Better Business Bureaus have reported receiving consumer complaints about a new type of pyramid scheme cropping up across the country. A typical ad for this new scam begins, "Would you spend $100 to generate $10,000 in less than 12 months? . . . See for yourself how to obtain a truly viable income opportunity in the exploding new industry of prepaid phone cards!" Those who respond are asked to pay a substantial fee to become a distributor of prepaid long-distance phone cards (cards usually sold in $5, $10, and $20 denominations) containing toll-free numbers and personal identification codes that make it possible to place long-distance calls from a pay phone without depositing money.

Many solicitations offering a "get-rich-quick" opportunity in phone card sales are simply pyramid schemes. Their focus is not on card sales but on the alleged quick profits to be earned by selling the right to recruit others. Telecard Network (TCN) is a prime example. In 1996 authorities cited the company for using prepaid phone cards as the basis of a pyramid operation. The firm's promotional literature offered prospective distributors the opportunity to earn

$10,000 within twelve months for a $100 investment. In fact not only were these earning claims excessive, but TCN was taking in most of its money by enlisting new salespeople, not through the sale of phone cards.

In May 1997 the New York Attorney General's Office assessed a record fine of approximately $350,000 against Destiny Telecomm, a California-based, multilevel marketing company for operating an illegal pyramid scheme in New York. Destiny sold prepaid calling cards, beeper services, voice mail, and home- and cellular-telephone services. But most of the company's profits appeared to be generated through a pyramid scheme that was built on layer upon layer of new recruits.

Still other BBBs have warned consumers about "gifting network" or friends network" operations that invite potential investors to confidential meetings and then offer them an opportunity to join the network (with an initial investment of anywhere from $100 to $2,000. About 400 people attend each meeting and they can buy in to differently priced tables with fifteen people at each one. The "giving" or "sharing" network is an obvious pyramid operation, according to one BBB representative, designed so that "volunteers" make initial investments. Eventually, the volunteers were moved into higher positions in the network. Describing one "giving" network, a BBB representative said that despite the plan's claims, "The network was an illegal endless chain because it was based on making money by paying money to get in and then recruiting more people to do the same. There was no product given for the money invested."

One new trend has been the use of the Internet to promote both Ponzi and pyramid schemes. "There's an alarming irony in this," noted a Federal Trade Commission (FTC) source. "Ten years ago, pyramid scams were all but a thing of the past. Today, we have a new marketplace, the Internet. . . . And here come the pyramid scams again, as old as Methuselah, disguised in high-tech electronic garb and new-age jargon, trying to make a comeback." The FTC also is doing its best to curtail that attempted comeback. In 1996 securities officials and law enforcement officials launched a massive surveil-lance operation designed to identify and discourage web site operators pro-moting illegal pyramid operations (see "Surfing for Pyramids" in chapter 10, "On-line Investment Fraud").

In fact, *all* pyramid schemes—whether promoted through print ads, telemar-keting, face-to-face recruitment, or on-line offers—are not only fraudulent but illegal. Even when a scam is identified and closed down, it is difficult to prose-cute the swindlers. For one thing, the initial promoters often are long gone by the time the authorities learn that a swindle is in progress. Then too, few victims are willing to come forward and make their gullibility public knowledge, espe-cially after realizing that they have little chance of getting their money back.

Be Informed About Pyramids

These basic precautionary guidelines can help you avoid being exploited by pyramid scheme promoters, according to NASAA and the BBB.

1. Start-up costs for investing in a pyramid scheme may not be substantial, but you may be pressured into becoming a "distributor." Remember that pyramid promoters make most of their profit by signing up new recruits.

2. Find out if the company will buy back inventory. Legitimate companies should be willing to buy back at least 80 percent of required inventory purchases; some state laws require 90 percent buy backs.

3. Consider whether there is a legitimate consumer market for the products or services. If the company seems to be making its money by recruiting alone, stay away.

4. Before investing, get all the facts about the company, its officers, and its products or services. Obtain written copies of the marketing plan, sales literature, and other literature. Do not assume, though, that official-look-ing documents are legitimate; investigate and verify all information. Also check with others who have had experience with the company and its products or services.

5. To check out a company, contact your state securities agency, local police department or district attorney's office, state attorney general's office, or local Better Business Bureau. You also may want to contact the Direct Selling Foundation (see Appendix C), a national trade association representing legitimate direct sales companies, including multilevel marketing companies.

The Funnel Scam

Pyramid scams seem to go in cycles. When one is shut down, a new and improved version surfaces. The following case is just another twist on a formula that has circulated around the country again and again.

It all started in the home of an employee of a Las Vegas public agency. When the employee's daughter, who lived out of state, came for a visit, she brought along a get-rich-quick scheme. Recruitment efforts focused on employees of public agencies such as the school system, prison system, fire department, and police department. The first person recruited in each organization was someone of local stature, whose membership added credibility to the scheme. That person served as spokesperson at numerous "invitation only" meetings, during which the scam was promoted and cash investments solicited.

Each new member was required to pay $2,000 and recruit two more people to do the same. When the inverted pyramid, which organizers called a "funnel," had accumulated eight people across the top, the person at the bottom was paid $16,000. The funnel then split into two with one more level of recruitment required before the second two people would be paid.

For several weeks the funnel scheme spread like wildfire with new members enthusiastically contributing as they witnessed the spokesperson receiving large sums of cash at each meeting. What these eager participants did not realize was that every pyramid scheme quickly hits a saturation point. At the second level of the funnel scam, thirty people had to contribute for the top three to be paid. For all of the original fifteen people in the first funnel to be paid, 256 people had to lose $2,000 each.

When officials of regulatory agencies finally learned about the scheme, press releases were sent out, warning the public that involvement in a pyramid operation is not only financially risky but also illegal. The Nevada Securities Division and Attorney General's Office conducted a joint investigation that resulted in criminal charges being filed against one of the original promoters. Civil suits were filed against several of the other promoters in the pyramid scheme.

Chapter 9

Boiler Rooms

Hello, Mr. Smith. How are you today? I'm glad to hear that, because you're going to feel even better when I tell you about the government's big new land program in Montana. Have you read about it or heard about it on television?

I see. Well, that's because it's too new for most people to know about. But out here—I'm calling from Cody, Wyoming—we're all very excited about the big new opportunities for investment and future profits.

I should explain who "we" are. We're PLUS—Profitable Land Utilization Service—one of the gold-chip firms of the West. We work directly with the government in the sale of land to a limited list of customers who want to make sure *they put their money only into sound, profitable investments. And what could be better than good land?*

What has happened—and I'm sure you'll be hearing more and more about this—is that the United States Bureau of Land Management is being forced to auction off some of its most valuable properties in several national parks as part of the new deficit reduction package. We've been fortunate to acquire thousands of acres of rights and are offering choice sites as investments to our selected customers.

Now, there's no commitment on your part, but if I can promise to show you some facts that could be very profitable to you, wouldn't you like to know how a very small investment at this time could at least quadruple your money in less than two years?

Now you're talking! I'll get some literature off to you in the very next mail out of Cody and let you see for yourself how really big the potential is. . . .

Reaching Out to "Touch" Someone

You are all too familiar with those irritating phone solicitations for everything from storm windows and aluminum siding to low-cost magazine subscriptions and bargain burglar alarm systems. Conditioned by experience to react with a decisive "no" to persistent telephone salespeople, you feel comfortably assured that you would never—absolutely not ever—fall for a sales pitch aimed at getting you to put several thousand dollars into land or some other investment. Or would you?

The unfortunate fact of the matter is that many thousands of individuals who thought themselves immune to fraudulent sales pitches have been duped by smooth-talking salespeople operating out of small offices known as "boiler rooms." The majority of telephone sales calls are made by legitimate businesses offering legitimate products or services. However, a large and seemingly infinite number of fraudulent telemarketers, playing on the universal interest in getting great financial returns for very little risk, swindle unwary investors out of billions of dollars every year. These con artists use clever dialogue and high-sounding terms to promote not only land but oil and gas leases, tax avoidance partnerships, coins, precious metals such as gold and silver, strategic metals such as chromium and indium, and stock—particularly cheap stock in emerging companies. They may promise 20 to 30 percent returns on an investment in gemstones that in actuality are of low to commercial grade and worth one-tenth of the selling price. They may promote a bogus new business opportunity (see chapter 1), penny stocks (see chapter 3), applications for wireless cable TV licenses (chapter 4), time-shares (chapter 7), or art prints (see below). The list of convincing and imaginative schemes goes on and on. The lures always include assurances that you can take the next step with absolutely no commitments, see resounding results quickly, and get your money back at any time if you are not satisfied with the deal.

One Better Business Bureau official reported that by the time relatives and the BBB intervened, an elderly victim was devastated by his loss of $59,000 to unscrupulous telemarketers. Another senior couple lost nearly $20,000 to a firm selling memberships in a camp-ground club. Fraudulent telemarketing schemes are consistently among the top complaints tracked by our Bureau, the official pointed out, emphasizing that consumers need to be careful when dealing with unsolicited marketers who ask for personal or financial information over the telephone and employ high pressure tactics.

Curiosity alone precipitates many victims into action when they agree over the phone to look at the promoter's "literature." Before they know it, they get a second phone call, this time ostensibly from the "manager" or a "partner" of the firm.

One of my salesmen, Bob Jones, said he had talked with you about our big land opportunity in Montana. Well, I've got exciting news for you because the acreage we obtained turned out to be on a lovely lake in the mountains, the choice site for a plush resort devel-opment. What we bought and can offer at a very low price will obvi-ously go at premium prices. Right now, in fact, one of the biggest recreational developers in the West is starting to bid on the adjacent acreage. So we have to act fast!

Did you receive our literature? Well, look at the map on page two and you'll see why I'm so excited about what we can offer our cus-tomers. We figure conservatively that an investment of only $5,000 would net you $25,000 or more in less than eighteen months with no risk. . . .

The phrase "boiler rooms" originated in the 1920s when telephones were first used in the promoting of worthless stocks by groups of salespeople crammed into crowded, low-rent offices as hot as the room from which their name is derived. The term "bucket shops" has also been used for this kind of operation, but there is a small distinction. While boiler-room operators are engaged in the high-pressure peddling of actual stocks and other investments of dubious value, the bucket-shop operator accepts a client's money without ever buying or selling the securities the client orders. This con artist simply pockets the money, gambling on the chance that the customer will pick a los-ing investment. When too many customers "invest" in securities whose value rises, the operator simply closes shop and moves to a new location.

The fraudulent telemarketer's modus operandi has become greatly refined with the use of computer-generated prospect lists and the perfection of scripts weaving together facts and falsehoods in a pitch tailored to induce a positive response. "Telescammers" are skilled liars, well versed in ways to make them-selves sound enthusiastic, sincere, honest, and credible. Depending on where they got your name, they may know your age, occupation, education, income, marital status, hobbies, and habits—information they use to establish credibili-ty and lower your sales resistance. The first thing most victims say when they realize they have been scammed is, "The caller sounded so believable."

Voice-switching may be another part of the boiler-room act. The sales pitch is suddenly interrupted by a supposed officer of the firm eager to tell you about a late-breaking development that can mean even more profits for investors. It is not unusual for some boiler-room promoters to use sound effects and other devices to heighten the excitement and give the listener the impression that the call is coming from a large Wall Street trading room where the action is fast and furious.

Two former phone scammers have described the techniques used to motivate them to rip off ever-larger quotas of prospects. One was to pin $500 in bills on the boiler-room wall, right over the bank of phones. The prize went to the salesperson who roped in the largest number of victims that day. In another rented room crammed with desks and phones, all the salespeople were instructed to stand while making their fevered pitches. One man wore a gorilla suit; another heightened the selling frenzy by taking an occasional spin around the room in his motorcycle.

Long-Distance "Operators"

It is impossible to measure the size or scope of boiler-room operations in the United States, since scammers use temporary offices, move frequently, and switch from one investment field to another, depending on the popularity and allure of each market. Complaints logged by the Telemarketing Fraud Database from callers to a national consumer assistance hotline come in at the rate of about 15,000 to 16,000 a year—and those represent only the small sampling of defrauded consumers who complain. The U.S. Congress estimates that American consumers lose more than $40 billion a year to telemarketing fraud. The National Consumers League, which operates a clearinghouse on consumer fraud, puts annual losses across North America at about $60 billion.

In the recent past there may have been as many as a hundred boiler rooms employing some 2,000 salespeople in Florida alone. However, the figures and locations keep changing. California, New York, and Las Vegas have

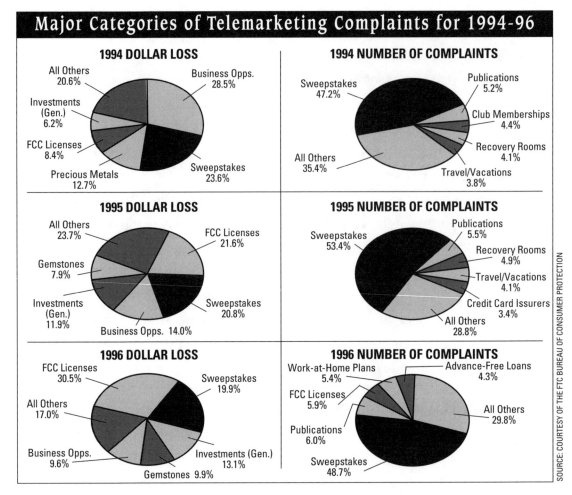

Major Categories of Telemarketing Complaints for 1994-96

1994 DOLLAR LOSS
- All Others 20.6%
- Investments (Gen.) 6.2%
- FCC Licenses 8.4%
- Precious Metals 12.7%
- Business Opps. 28.5%
- Sweepstakes 23.6%

1994 NUMBER OF COMPLAINTS
- Sweepstakes 47.2%
- Publications 5.2%
- Club Memberships 4.4%
- Recovery Rooms 4.1%
- Travel/Vacations 3.8%
- All Others 35.4%

1995 DOLLAR LOSS
- All Others 23.7%
- Gemstones 7.9%
- Investments (Gen.) 11.9%
- Business Opps. 14.0%
- FCC Licenses 21.6%
- Sweepstakes 20.8%

1995 NUMBER OF COMPLAINTS
- Sweepstakes 53.4%
- Publications 5.5%
- Recovery Rooms 4.9%
- Travel/Vacations 4.1%
- Credit Card Issuers 3.4%
- All Others 28.8%

1996 DOLLAR LOSS
- FCC Licenses 30.5%
- All Others 17.0%
- Business Opps. 9.6%
- Gemstones 9.9%
- Investments (Gen.) 13.1%
- Sweepstakes 19.9%

1996 NUMBER OF COMPLAINTS
- Work-at-Home Plans 5.4%
- FCC Licenses 5.9%
- Publications 6.0%
- Sweepstakes 48.7%
- Advance-Free Loans 4.3%
- All Others 29.8%

SOURCE: COURTESY OF THE FTC BUREAU OF CONSUMER PROTECTION

also been popular sites for these fly-by-night operations. One such case occurred in October 1996 when the New York Attorney General's Office succeeded in securing 100% restitution for more than 200 victims of a multi-state investment scam in which Mugs Plus, Inc., a manufacturer of souvenir mugs and t-shirts, targeted senior citizens. Nearly $1 million will be returned to investors as a result. Mugs Plus conducted an intensive telemarketing campaign selling stock in a defunct New Jersey company.

In a coordinated effort federal law enforcement agencies and their counterparts at the state and local levels have joined together to combat telemarketing fraud. Several Better Business Bureaus also cooperated with the Federal Bureau of Investigation (FBI) by providing information to track down the operators of fraudulent telemarketing scams. The FBI's nationwide sting, called **Operation Disconnect**, targeted 123 telemarketing operations in thirteen states, resulting in the arrest of 240 individuals.

In 1996 **Project Jackpot**, a joint state and federal investigation coordinated by the Federal Trade Commission (FTC), resulted in enforcement actions against fifty-six telemarketing firms and seventy-nine individuals in seventeen states. The telescammers targeted in this operation fraudulently offered "valuable" prizes or awards to consumers to induce them to purchase products. Other major enforcement actions targeted at alleged fraudulent telemarketers have included **Project Roadblock** (see chapter 4, "High-Tech and FCC License Scams"); **Project Telesweep**, a joint state-federal sweep on telemarketers engaged in business opportunity fraud; **Operation Senior Sentinel**, a state-FBI operation against boiler-room frauds that were aimed primarily at older Americans; and the **Chattanooga Telemarketing Fraud Project**, an operation that sought to bring criminal sanctions against fraudulent telemarketers, leading to restitution orders of more than $2.7 million. These and other high-profile enforcement actions were carried out to enforce the **Telemarketing Sales Rule**, adopted in 1995 (see below).

In July 1997 NASAA and the FTC announced a campaign of enforcement and consumer education, dubbed **Project Field of Schemes**, to stop telemarketing schemes involving new types of investment fraud involving such areas as movies production, Internet "shopping malls," and snail ranching—as well as old standbys like pyramid schemes and conventional telemarketing fraud. "Swindlers are becoming more creative in how they steal people's money," Mark Griffin, president of NASAA, said in a statement. "Losses from these nontraditional investment schemes are outpacing the amount defrauded from consumers in all other kinds of telemarketing scams."

The law enforcement effort, led by securities regulators from twenty-one states and two Canadian provinces and the FTC, had been under way for six months. It included 61 cases, some of which involved criminal prosecution.

Examples of what Griffin called "a contemptible array of investment scams"—most offered through unsolicited telephone calls included: allegedly worthless oil and gas drilling in Kentucky; digital fingerprint technology in Indiana; ostrich farming in Idaho; snail ranching in Iowa and Nebraska; retirement investments for the clergy in Maryland; interest in frozen embryos from a cow named Missy Cool in Ohio; basketball training machine investments in Massachusetts; ATM terminals that also charge and recharge prepaid phone cards in Missouri; and in Pennsylvania $25,000 "commercial promissory notes" to build clinics in Hungary, a water treatment plant in the Congo, and roads in Bosnia.

Mark Griffin had this advice for consumers if they get calls promoting similar deals: "Keep one hand on your wallet and hang up the phone."

"If we can alert more consumers to the tell-tale signs of fraudulent investments, we will help reduce the power of unscrupulous operators who prey on gullible investors," stated James Bast, CBBB president.

Fraud Across the Border

In the wake of the crackdowns, many fraudulent telemarketers have packed their bags and moved north to Canada, creating new challenges for U.S. law enforcement. In 1996 there were an estimated five hundred telemarketing firms based in Canada but targeting potential victims in the United States. This marked a dramatic growth in cross-border telephone fraud.

In one case, United States and Canadian officials brought indictments against forty-four gemstone telemarketers who operated out of Toronto and bilked U.S. investors out of $35 million. In another 1997 case, the Federal Trade Commission obtained a court order temporarily halting a credit card laundering service that allowed Canadian telemarketers to bilk U.S. consumers out of tens of millions of dollars by deceptively selling foreign lottery shares. This was the first FTC action under the credit-card laundering provisions of the **Telemarketing Sales Rules**.

The Telemarketing Sales Rule

Adopted by the FTC in 1995, the **Telemarketing Sales Rule** requires telemarketers to give potential customers key information to guide their investment and buying decisions. When telemarketers phone you, they must promptly disclose, among other facts, that the call is a sales call; the nature and total cost of any goods or services being sold; and the risk, liquidity, earnings potential, or profitability of any investment being offered. The rule also places restrictions on *when* telemarketers may phone. It prohibits sales calls before 8 a.m. and after 9 p.m., your time, and, if you ask a telemarketer not to call you anymore, the rule makes it illegal for that person or firm to phone you again.

With a few exceptions, the **Telemarketing Sales Rule** covers all companies and individuals taking part in any plan, program, or campaign to sell goods or services through interstate telephone calls. According to law enforcement authorities, the restrictions and penalties will make the rule a major step toward reducing fraud. One consumer affairs official sees the law as "a more concerted and unified effort to stop the deception and fraud of some telemarketers. . . . It sets up the rules. It's a federal law the states can use."

Another favorite scam for Canada-based boiler rooms involves the promotion of fraudulent loan application services. Posing as a loan company, the scammer promises consumers that he can obtain loans and then asks applicants for advance loan processing fees ranging from $25 to hundreds of dollars. The company pockets the advance fees, often failing even to process the loan applications. Con artists at other cross-border boiler-room shops have posed as employees of the U.S. Internal Revenue Service or Customs Service. Phoning consumers with the news that they have won a prize in a foreign lottery or sweepstakes, these con artists persuade their victims to pay exorbitant "import duties" before the prize—which often turns out to be of poor quality or nonexistent—is released.

Other cross-border telemarketing frauds that investors should be wary of involve:

- Telemarketers of indium, a strategic metal used in making computer screens, and
- Promoters of "prime bank notes," sometimes offered as "standing

letters of credit" or "promissory bank notes," allegedly issued by well-known or off-shore banks. The promoters claim that notes are safe and pay much higher than market returns. However, the notes may be difficult to explain and understand. And more importantly, they may be worthless and fraudulent. (See chapter 6, Investing Overseas.)

In an effort to strengthen cooperation in the crackdown on deceptive advertising and telemarketing, the FTC and Canadian law enforcement officials formed the **Task Force on Cross-Border Deceptive Marketing Practices**. The task force focuses on identifying suspect cross-border operations and fostering cooperation and reciprocal efforts to combat them more effectively.

Another important element of U.S.–Canadian efforts to combat international telemarketing fraud has been **Project PhoneBusters**, a joint operation of Canadian law enforcement agencies, consumer affairs organizations, and Canadian Better Business Bureaus. **Project PhoneBusters** has become the central source for telemarketing complaints throughout Canada. It is estimated that in a single year, **Project PhoneBusters'** operators prevented 25 percent of complainants from being victimized, for an estimated savings of approximately $8.5 million. Intelligence information collected by phone operators fielding calls from consumers contacted by fraudulent telemarketers is shared with U.S. law enforcers, and that data has been a valuable tool in evaluating the extent and effects of this type of fraud. The goals of **Project PhoneBusters** include the prosecution of Canada-based individuals involved in telemarketing fraud, both under Canadian laws and, where feasible, by U.S. agencies through extradition.

Hook, Line, and Sucker

How does a boiler-room operator select *you* as a hot prospect? Your name may be on a computerized list of consumers who have inquired about legitimate stocks and other investments. Or you may have stuck your neck out in the past by answering one of the promoter's own direct mail, newspaper, or magazine ads seeking investors who would like to "double their income" or "ensure a worry-free retirement." Boiler rooms also exchange or sell each other "sucker lists," knowing that people who get hooked by one scheme are likely to invest in another, as long as they can be reached before the awful truth dawns on them.

According to the BBB, NASAA and FTC, the typical sales pitch of a fraudulent telemarketer includes these elements:

- The assurance that you have been specially selected to participate in an unusual investment opportunity.
- A believable message combining truths, half-truths, and lies.
- The guarantee of large and rapid profits.
- The claim that virtually no risk is involved.
- The requirement that money be paid immediately because the "market is moving."

Telescammers are resourceful in explaining why their investment opportunity is a sure thing. They may claim high-level financial connections or inside information; and they may offer a "guarantee," a certificate of authenticity, or the promise to buy back the investment after a certain period. To close the sale quickly, con artists may quote phony statistics or misrepresent the significance of a current event. There is always an urgent reason why you must make your decision *right now*. As part of the "urgency" pitch, the scammer may offer to send someone to your home or office to pick up the money or insist on the use of overnight mail or some other method to get your funds quickly.

A Second Bite

"I know you have been the victim of fraud, and I can help you get your money back."

If you have taken the bait and lost money to a fraudulent telemarketer,

Art Print Scams

During the past few years, news stories about the dramatic escalation in value of works of art by noted masters have led to a rash of speculative purchasing by amateur art collectors. While few investors have aspirations of finding any bargains in Van Goghs or Cézannes, many are lured by the opportunity to buy lithographs, engravings, and other fine art prints by celebrated artists such as Salvador Dali, Pablo Picasso, Marc Chagall, and Joan Miró.

Even more aware of the profit potential than would-be art collectors are fraudulent telemarketers, who have built a thriving business on the sale of counterfeit artwork. Many of these bogus pieces are copies of images created by well-known artists, which are produced without the artist's knowledge or authorization and carry a forged signature. Photomechanical techniques have made it possible to transform high-quality color photographs of valuable works of art into lithographs or silk-screen prints that closely resemble the originals. Other bogus works are counterfeits produced in the style of well-known artists. In still other cases, the artwork may be authentic but have far less value and investment potential than buyers are led to believe.

Fraudulent telemarketers use various tactics to trick consumers into paying inflated prices for counterfeit artwork. A telescammer may offer you a "fabulous" opportunity to obtain a limited-edition print that will be an "excellent investment." You may be told that a famous artist is near death and that you should buy now, since the value of the art will increase dramatically after the artist's death. Often you are promised a trial examination period with a money-back guarantee. If you are taken in by the sales pitch, you could end up paying anywhere from $500 to $10,000 or more for artwork valued at no more than $50.

One boiler-room "art gallery" in New York, whose operators were convicted at trial, was described by witnesses in court as "little more than a vestibule with several prints on the wall and two rooms with telephones." According to an undercover agent who posed as a salesperson, about ten con artists used the phones to solicit

expect to hear just such a line from another telescammer . . . or even from the one that has already fleeced you. Consumers who have been victimized often are placed on "sucker lists" created, bought, and sold by unscrupulous promoters. "Recovery" or "reload" scams seek to trick these victims into believing that "this time" they will win the "grand prize," or at least recover their investment. Most often, however, they simply end up losing more money.

customers for the gallery, but no prospective customers ever walked in. Customers received fancy certificates of authenticity with their purchases. One customer testified that he had three such certificates for what proved to be reproductions worth about one-thirtieth of the $7,000 he had paid.

In another art fraud case, a doctor paid a total of $125,000 over a period of several years for twenty-one works that salespeople assured him were original, limited-edition lithographs. The doctor never set foot in the gallery from which he made his purchases; all business was conducted by phone. By the time he tried to resell the art through Sotheby's auction house and discovered that the total worth of his bogus lithographs was actually about $2,000, the gallery was long gone and the owners could not be traced.

Although there is no foolproof way to protect yourself against fraud if you invest in art, the FTC offers consumers these suggestions:

✔ *Get professional advice.* Counterfeit prints often are so well produced that few laypersons can distinguish a fake. It is important to consult a reputable expert, such as an art appraiser or museum curator, before finalizing the purchase of any artwork attributed to a well-known artist.

✔ *Be extremely careful about buying artwork over the telephone.* Check with your local Better Business Bureau to determine whether complaints have been lodged against the company contacting you. But be aware that, since many fraudulent telemarketing companies frequently change their names, an absence of complaints is no guarantee that you are dealing with a reputable firm.

✔ *Be skeptical of authenticity claims.* A certificate of authenticity or written appraisal is only as good as the firm backing it up. Also avoid being taken in by dealers who refer you to "art appraisers" who are on the dealer's payroll.

✔ *Be suspicious of high-pressure sales tactics and promises of great investment returns.* Ask yourself this question: If the investment is so good, why is a total stranger making such an effort to sell it to me?

Reloaders may claim to represent a government agency, consumer organization, or private company that, for a fee or a donation to a specified charity, will work to recover lost funds. Some scammers say they are holding money for you. Others offer to file the paperwork needed to process your claim, or claim they can have your name placed at the top of a list for reimbursement.

To avoid being victimized by a recovery scam, be aware that some local government agencies and consumer organizations do provide assistance to consumers who have lost money to fraud. However, these groups never *guarantee* to get all or some of your money back and they do not charge a fee. Before using any recovery services by phone, ask what specific services the company provides. Do not ever "purchase" such services. Ask for written materials about the company and check it out with a call to local law enforcement, state securities and consumer agencies and your local Better Business Bureau. And do not give out your credit card number, checking account number, or other personal financial information to an unknown business or individual, no matter how persuasive. These precautions may not help you recover money lost to a con artist, but they can prevent the scammer from taking a second bite out of your hard-earned resources.

> *Hello, Mr. Smith. How are you today?*
> *Fine. That's just fine. Now for the good news. I'm calling about the geological data I sent you on PDQ Treasure Mines, Ltd. Well, you can double the production figures. I've just come back from a visit to our holdings in northern Saskatchewan and you wouldn't believe the way those chaps up there are panning the gold. . . .*

Breaking the Boiler-Room Connection

Whenever you receive a telephone call offering any form of investment "opportunity," the BBB and NASAA advise you to follow these tips.

1. ***Be skeptical about any unsolicited phone calls about investments.*** If you buy investments by telephone, especially from out-of-state people you don't know, you may find it difficult or impossible to get your money back if the deal turns sour.

2. ***Do not let the caller pressure you into making a hurried decision.*** High pressure sales tactics are a red flag. If a telemarketer pushes you to invest *now*, hang up the phone.

3. ***Do not make an investment until you clearly understand all***

the details of the plan. The greater your confusion, the greater the chance that you will be swindled.

4. *Ask for written information about the company, the salesperson, and the investment.* Ask what state or federal agencies the firm is registered with or regulated by, and verify the information with those agencies. Also check out the seller and the investment opportunity with your state's securities agency and local Better Business Bureau.

5. *Do not part with your money until you have consulted with your accountant, banker, lawyer, financial adviser, or other knowledgeable professional.* If a salesperson tries to discourage you from seeking a second opinion, consider that a tip-off to fraud.

6. *Be wary of testimonials.* Fraudulent companies may invent tributes or pay people to claim the firm's investments brought them wealth.

7. *Be cautious when answering advertisements in newspapers and other publications that give little information about the seller other than an 800 number.* By responding, you may unwittingly be inviting telescammers to call.

8. *Never send cash through the mail or hand it to a messenger sent by the salesperson.* Also do not give out any personal financial information over the phone unless you are absolutely certain you are dealing with a reputable company.

9. *If in doubt, do not invest.* If you cannot get solid information about the company and the investment, do not risk your money.

10. *If you suspect you have been contacted by a phone scammer, notify your state securities agency and local Better Business Bureau.* Prompt action may help you recover any funds you have invested, and it may protect less wary investors from swindlers.

Chapter 10

On-Line Investment Fraud

Just a decade ago, the on-line world was the nearly exclusive province of government agencies and academics linked together through the decentralized collection of computer networks that came to be known as the Internet. Millions of people now have entered that informal web of computer networks, and millions more have gone on-line by subscribing to commercial on-line services. Cyberspace—the on-line world—can be a complicated and confusing place, but its appeal is easy to understand. Going on-line opens up a new world to consumers who use their personal computers to access messages posted on computer bulletin boards, enter live discussion groups, exchange electronic mail, play games, read publications, conduct research, and buy goods and services.

One of the most powerful magnets drawing consumers to cyberspace has been the growing number of bulletin boards and discussion groups devoted to investment topics. This trend offers investors both new opportunities and new challenges. By offering a wealth of instantly accessible research data and financial news, the on-line world has the potential to educate consumers, helping them to become wiser investors. At the same time, just as millions of inexperienced newcomers crowd onto the information superhighway, investment swindlers have seized on cyberspace as a new haven for their illegal schemes.

Many of the messages posted on investment bulletin boards and "chat rooms" offer general stock-picking advice and discussions of other investment possibilities. However, an increasing number of investment-specific messages tout specific stocks, money-making enterprises, and service providers, often offering further details via e-mail and toll-free phone numbers. Households with access to the Internet and/or to the major on-line services are being exposed to hundreds of fraudulent and abusive investment schemes, which have included the following:

- An "e-mail chain letter" scheme promoted by a San Antonio man and accomplices around the country lured investors with the line: "How to make big money from your home computer," according to a cease and desist action filed by the New Jersey Bureau of Securities. Promoters claimed that investors could "turn $5 into $60,000 in just three to six weeks." How? Simply by sending $1 to each of five people on an on-line list, adding their own name to that list, and then posting messages explaining the scheme on ten different computer bulletin board sites. In practice, the promotion was just an electronic version of the classic pyramid scheme, barred under federal and state laws.
- On-line hyping of a Canadian company whose stock was traded over-the-counter in Canada outside established exchanges pushed

the stock price from 20 cents to $1.40 in a single month. In this "pump and dump" scheme, promoters posted on-line messages claiming that the company owned a Zaire diamond mine where a major strike had been made. Said one on-line observer: "The company's story was made to sound like the biggest get-rich-quick prospect this side of Mars, and a lot of naive investors began buying . . . until the Alberta Exchange halted trading [and began] investigating the manipulation of the share price."

• A teenager looking for fast cash created a bond offering for half a million dollars and placed an ad on the Internet. Prospective investors in an eel-farming operation the young man called "Golden Waters Productions" were told to expect returns of 20 percent with very little risk. Unable to find investment authorities to endorse his business, the teenager made up some names and quoted fictitious financial experts who extolled his offering as "virtually risk-free" and "the best bond investment of this century!" The Securities and Exchange Commission shut this promoter down before his nonexistent company could take in any money.

• The Texas State Securities Board investigated a case in which one Austin-area retiree sent a total of $10,000 to an out-of-state con artist who used a major computer bulletin board service to promote himself as a skilled money manager. In fact, the swindler, who was not a licensed stockbroker or investment adviser, simply pocketed the investor's money.

Cyberspace Schemes

On-line computing enables individuals to reach more people more easily, quickly, and inexpensively than ever before—and investment swindlers have been quick to take advantage of this powerful new medium. Even the fastest talking boiler-room operator would be hard-pressed to make more than 150 telemarketing pitches in a day. But that same operator can reach hundreds of thousands of individuals simply by posting a message on a computer bulletin board or joining the discussions in an on-line chat room. As one veteran state securities agency official observed, "In my 32 years of investigating fraud, this is by far the greatest money-making machine for scammers that I have ever seen."

The medium may be new, but the message is all too familiar. Many of the investment fraud and abuse problems now cropping up in cyberspace have been in circulation elsewhere for years. Others take advantage of the on-line world's vast audience to promote new high-tech scams. The following are among the most prominent cyberschemes.

Pyramid Schemes

"What if you paid . . . $250 a month which produced a minimum of $5,250 income each month for you, while you simply watched?" That is how one Washington-based company promoted a classic pyramid scheme, inducing thousands of unwary consumers to fork over enrollment fees of between $250 and $1,750. In pyramid schemes, participants attempt to profit solely by recruiting new members into the program. Early entrants may make some money, but most people lose their investment as the pool of new participants dries up and the pyramid collapses. (For a further discussion of pyramid schemes, see chapter 8, "Ponzis and Pyramids.") This type of scam is well suited to the world of on-line computing, with its easy and relatively inexpensive access to many thousands of potential victims.

Pump and Dump Scams

Most commercial bulletin board services allow subscribers to post messages under a screen name or alias, even under multiple aliases. This opens the door to abuse by schemers seeking to run up the price of a stock for their own profit. Acting alone or with accomplices, a company insider, a broker, a marketing executive, or even just a large shareholder can post numerous bulletin board messages under different aliases calculated to spark interest in a little-known, thinly traded stock. Often the promoter claims to have inside information about impending announcements, product innovations, or new contracts. As unwary investors read about

Surfing for Pyramid Schemes

On just one day in late 1996, federal, state, and local law enforcement officials, including NASAA members, surfing the Internet located 770 web sites bearing the telltale signs of possible pyramid operations. **Internet Pyramid Surf Day** was part of an effort coordinated by the Federal Trade Commission (FTC) to put on-line schemers on notice. "The Internet is not going to be a new marketplace where scam artists roam free," an FTC official declared. "We've sent the message, 'Clean up your act or close down your site.'"

Law enforcement participants in the **Surf Day** operation located web sites that posted possible pyramid scams and sent the site operators e-mail messages warning that pyramid schemes are illegal and describing the characteristics of illegal pyramids. Suspect web sites will be revisited in the future, and if evidence suggests that they are illegal operations, further actions will be taken. "We are doing this," noted the FTC, "to help educate Internet entrepreneurs about the law on pyramids and to let deliberate, determined scammers know that we're determined to enforce the law."

The Better Business Bureau system also participated in Surf Day by distributing educational materials through its Web Page and network of BBBs to advise consumers on how to identify pyramid schemes and other on-line scams.

In April 1997 NASAA and the FTC announced the results of a second Internet surveillance campaign, this time targeting phony business opportunity schemes advertised on the Internet. During **Business Opportunity Surf Day**, in March 1997, numerous law enforcement officials at the state, federal, and international levels surfed the Internet for companies promoting business through false or unsubstantiated earnings claims. NASAA and the FTC sent notices to 191 suspect websites, warning them that claims regarding earnings must be backed up by solid evidence. When the sites were later revisited, officials found that 23 percent had been changed or taken down. The remaining sites were downloaded and preserved for possible future use by law enforcement.

According to NASAA and the FTC, a major aim of **Business Opportunity Surf Day** was "to educate entrepreneurs who might not know what the law requires in the way of substantiation for earnings promises. We also hope that this brand of 'community policing' on the Net will chase fraudulent operators off the Internet." The FTC and the states planned to make Internet surfing a regular part of their law enforcement efforts.

the "great opportunity" and buy shares, the stock price rises and the insiders sell their shares at a profit in the rising market. Often, when the hype-fueled stock price inevitably begins to falter, promoters blame unnamed short sellers and urge unsuspecting investors to "dollar average" and keep buying shares at the falling prices. In one variation on this scheme, promoters hiding under the cloak of anonymity claim inside knowledge that a stock price is about to fall, then buy up shares as their self-fulfilling prophecy comes true.

Investment Adviser Misconduct

Unlicensed or unethical brokers or investment advisers may use cyberspace to rope in new clients through illegal assurances about potential returns on investments. One state securities agency investigated a woman who used a commercial bulletin board to offer her services as an investment adviser. Complaints from consumers around the country alerted the agency to the extreme claims the phony adviser was making about potential profits and to her possible mishandling of client accounts. In another case, a pair of promoters collected more than $3.5 million by promising to double clients' money in four months through investments in "prime bank" securities—a type of security that does not even exist.

Exotic Scams

Hundreds of highly suspect, unregistered investment deals have been promoted on-line, with these scams often targeted toward individuals who do not feel sophisticated enough to speculate in traditional stocks. Exotic schemes run the gamut from high-tech wireless cable television projects and bogus business opportunity schemes to investments in fictitious coconut plantations and eel farms. The FTC has brought charges against companies making false claims on-line about repairing consumers' credit records, offering to match consumers with private foundations with "billions of dollars" to give away, and promising astronomical profits in international investment ventures. Exotic schemes can be particularly costly to burned investors, with minimum investments often running $5,000 or more.

In 1997 the New York Attorney General's Office issued a cease and desist letter to Destiny Pictures, a California film production company, that offered stock in a low-budget movie over the Internet. Without looking to prevent the Internet as a legitimate way to raise capital, the Attorney General attempted to insure that those who seek to use this new medium comply with the appropriate laws and regulations. Likewise the California Department of Corporations took action in 1997 against a scheme involving the sale of nonexistent Internet sites in California. While another state securities agency investigated a publicly traded corporation whose offering materials on the Internet included "profiles" on the company that appeared to come from an independent source based upon the language within the profile report. However the company that prepared the profile report did not do any independent research or verification on the company. In fact the corporation had paid for the report to be written.

Unregistered Sales of Securities

Several state securities agencies have taken enforcement actions against promoters who have offered the sale of securities over the Internet, but have not properly registered the securities for sale in the state. They included:

- The Arizona Corporation Commission obtained a Consent to a Cease and Desist Order in November 1996 against two individuals and two companies after gold contracts in future gold mining production in Arizona were offered to residents over the Internet. The gold contracts were found to have been unregistered for sale in Arizona, the promoters were not licensed to sell securities in the state, and misrepresentations and omissions of material facts were found within the securities offering materials over the Internet.

- The Pennsylvania Securities Commission issued a Cease and Desist Order against two companies and the promoter in January 1997 for the sale of unregistered securities over the Internet, after a Pennsylvania resident responded via e-mail on America Online to the company's offer, and disclosure information about the company was then faxed to the resident.

- The Ohio Division of Securities issued a Cease and Desist Order in July 1997 against a promoter and a company that was offering real time sports wagering services and other gaming related products on the Internet after the securities were found to be unregistered in Ohio. The Web site home page of the company stated "Investors are encouraged to review our Prospectus," and directed Ohio residents to access investment information for common stock from another Web site.

- A state securities agency investigated a company that put an offering on the Internet that stated in the posted offering materials that it was "exempt from their state securities registration laws" and it was a "private offering." The Internet, according to the agency, offering could be construed to be an advertisement; therefore, any exemption from registration would not apply. It also would not be a private securities offering since anyone with access to the Internet in that state could read this information.

Steering Clear of Cyberfraud

There will never be enough "cybercops" to keep the far-flung on-line world free from fraud and abuse. That does not mean, though, that investors should avoid cyberspace. The following steps, according to NASAA and the BBB, can help you keep on guard when you go on-line.

1. ***Do not expect to get rich quick.*** When evaluating an investment you have learned about on-line, exercise the same caution and deliberation that you would bring to any unfamiliar investment

opportunity. The old rule "If it sounds too good to be true, it probably is" applies just as much to offers made in cyberspace as to those made through any other medium.

2. ***Download and print a hard copy of any on-line solicitation you are considering.*** This document may come in handy if problems develop later. Be sure to note the Internet address and date and time of the offer.

3. ***Do not assume that an on-line computer service polices its investment bulletin boards.*** The vast majority of services take a "hands-off" approach to screening claims made in message postings, and even those that do minimal policing cannot possibly keep up with the millions of messages posted each month. Remember, too, that anyone can set up a web site or advertise on-line, usually without any check on the legitimacy of their claims.

4. ***Never buy little-known, thinly traded stocks strictly on the basis of on-line hype.*** Low-volume stocks are the most susceptible to manipulation since their price can be moved through relatively small strategic trades. Even if a hyped stock starts to move up, proceed with caution—this may just be part of the overall manipulation scheme.

5. ***Be cautious about acting on the advice of individuals who hide their identity.*** The use of aliases on computer bulletin boards is intended to protect privacy, but it also can be exploited by con artists. People on-line may not be who they claim. What seems to be two or more different people talking up a stock may actually be a single individual with a personal interest in driving up its price through false information or baseless speculation. And an impressive-looking web site, complete with company logos stolen from a legitimate web site, can be the product of a laptop computer on the other side of the world, far from the jurisdiction of U.S. law enforcement and regulators.

6. *Do not get taken in by claims of "inside information" such as pending news releases, contract announcements, and innovative new products.* In cyberspace practically anyone can say anything. Despite the abundance of "hot tips" littered across bulletin boards and discussion groups, it is extremely unlikely that genuine insider information will be publicly broadcast on an investment bulletin board.

7. *Be skeptical about claims that an on-line stock hypester has personally checked out an investment.* One established tactic of investment schemers is to talk up companies, mining operations, and factories in remote corners of the country or the globe, where it can be impossible for the average investor to investigate or visit in person.

8. *Take the time to investigate outside sources of information on any investment you learn about on-line.* Check with a trusted financial adviser and always obtain written financial information, such as a prospectus, annual report, offering circular, and financial statements. Ask the on-line promoter where the firm is incorporated, and call the state's Secretary of State to verify that information. Also make sure that an investment opportunity and the person promoting it are properly registered with your state securities agency. Check out the growing number of on-line sites that monitor on-line scams, including those of the North American Securities Administrators Association (**http://www.nasaa.org**), the Better Business Bureau (**http://www.bbb.org**), the National Fraud and Information Center (**http://www.fraud.org**), the Securities and Exchange Commission (**http://www.sec.gov**), and the National Association of Securities Dealers (**http://www.nasdr.com**).

9. *If you think you have been duped, do not be embarrassed about complaining.* Early action increases your chances of getting

your money back and may prevent others from losing money. If you spot a potential on-line investment fraud, contact your state securities administrator, Better Business Bureau, the Federal Trade Commission, or the Securities Exchange Commission (see appendices).

BBB and NASAA On-Line

The Better Business Bureau provides instant access to business and consumer alerts as well as helpful resources through the BBB World Wide Web page (**http://www.bbb.org**). Plus, consumers can file complaints and access information and services on-line. The BBB web site is provided by the Council of Better Business Bureaus (CBBB) and the BBB system of more than 150 bureaus located throughout the United States and Canada.

BBB services on-line include:

- *Alerts and News:* The latest consumer warnings and other news from the BBB
- *Business Report Databases:* How to obtain a BBB report on a business
- *Charity Reports and Standards:* How to obtain a BBB report on a charity
- *Dispute Resolution:* How BBBs help resolve marketplace disputes and how to file on-line complaint forms
- *Resource Library:* BBB consumer buying guides and business publications
- *Locate a BBB:* Find the BBB serving your community
- *Programs and Services:* How BBBs work for businesses and consumers
- *Advertising Review Programs:* BBB programs to promote ethical advertising and selling practices
- *Membership Rosters and Information:* How and why to join the BBB, membership standards, and how to obtain membership rosters
- *Frequently Asked Questions:* About the BBB and the CBBB

• *BBB Online for an Ethical Marketplace*

In addition, the Better Business Bureau system offers **BBBOnLine** (**http://www.bbbonline.org**), an Internet service that provides consumers with an easy, trusted tool to separate the legitimate on-line offer from the dubious one. Activated in April 1997, the program gives consumers "right time, right place" information about companies that market products or services over the Internet and provides on-line advertisers with the means to display their commitment to ethical business and advertising practices.

Companies that commit to the high **BBBOnLine** program standards are authorized by the BBB to display a protected **BBBOnLine** seal in their on-line advertising. When consumers locate an on-line advertiser displaying the seal, they can click on the seal to be linked to a confirmation page demonstrating that the company is a legitimate participant in **BBBOnLine**. The consumer can then quickly pull up a BBB report on the company and return to the company's web site.

A key component of **BBBOnLine** is the on-site visit. To assure consumers that an advertiser's web site is supported by a functioning business, a BBB representative will visit the firm's place of business prior to accepting the company into the **BBBOnLine** program.

In the event of consumer, competitor, or BBB challenges regarding the truth and accuracy of an on-line claim, **BBBOnLine** participating companies are required to cooperate with an advertising self-regulation review program. **BBBOnLine** also gives consumers access to assistance in resolving disputes with businesses, including mediation and arbitration services. Links to **BBBOnLine** will be immediately deactivated in the event that any participating business fails to answer consumer complaints or otherwise refuses to comply with **BBBOnLine** standards. Additional information about the program is available at **http://www.bbbonline.org**.

NASAA has two services enabling the speedy and efficient fulfillment of consumer requests for a variety of information. An automated, toll-free telephone information retrieval system (1-888-84-NASAA) gives callers easy access to prerecorded information. Consumers also can phone the toll-free number to order NASAA publications through a fax-back/voice mail system.

A compendium of investor education materials is just a click away at NASAA's Internet site on the World Wide Web (**http://www.nasaa.org**). The site provides basic information about NASAA and includes a membership directory in the form of a map of North America and a pull-down menu. To obtain contact information, users can either click on a state, province, or territory from the map or choose a location from the pull-down list.

Although the primary purpose of the web site is investor education, sub-pages offer downloadable information on a variety of subjects.

NASAA on-line services include:

- ***Search Engine:*** A search engine built into the home page allows surfers to jump to the page or pages with information they are seeking simply by entering a key word or words.

- ***Investor Alerts:*** Over two dozen Investor Alerts are offered at no charge. These popular publications cover a wide range of topics from Penny Stock Fraud and Investing in Coins to the Renaissance of Ponzi Schemes.

- ***Downloadable Information:*** Information is provided regarding NASAA enforcement activities, legislative and media affairs, small business assistance, and franchise and business opportunities.

- ***Model Rules Page:*** Provides proposals that have been adopted by the membership and can be commented upon by members of the bar and the securities industry through e-mail to corporate office staff.

- ***Audio Clips:*** These clips are taken from NASAA video news releases, press conferences, and forums.

- ***Hyperlinks:*** Connect the NASAA site to the ever growing number of member web sites.

This is all part of the effort to make NASAA materials available to the widest audience possible.

Chapter 11

How To Select and Work With A Financial Planner

ever before have so many individuals, couples, families, and organizations invested their money in stocks, bonds, and other securities. For the most part, these investments have been financially rewarding, contributing to the general health of the economy and enabling many people to enjoy more comfortable lifestyles and provide security for the future.

One of the most exciting dramas on Wall Street has been the new-issue market, the process by which corporations of all sizes and types make it possible for the public to own shares in stocks and bonds in companies, individually and collectively. The volume in new issues has escalated to more than $155 billion annually, a significant amount of money even when viewed in the context of the $5.5 trillion traded annually in the equity trading market. Much of the drama of new-issue trading lies in the excitement of placing one's money in new and promising fields of endeavor, such as high-tech development, medical research, and computer innovations. But investing in a new company with no track record can be a gamble, resulting in either a substantial return or a resounding loss.

The gigantic world of new-issue investments is only one of a sometimes puzzling multitude of financial opportunities available to any who want to play the money game. In addition to the public issues, which must be processed through your state securities regulator and the federal Securities and Exchange Commission (SEC), an unknown number of investments are handled privately each year, often on little more than a handshake or through informal written papers. Most of these are stocks or some form of loan agreement in which the lender stands to profit if the project in question is successful. Many of the participants are not individuals but mutual fund organizations, insurance companies, or limited partnerships. Although private investing is often the realm of small companies, giant corporations sometimes initiate private issues to underwrite special objectives.

Add to this dazzling financial array the world of government bonds, the little-understood fields of commodity futures contracts, and the recent trend toward international investing, and the average investor is likely to be confused and unsure about the best way to put available resources to good use. It is no wonder that the financial planning industry has secured a solid position in the investment world and is growing at an explosive rate. Investors who are fortunate enough to have placed their future—or at least part of it—in the hands of a capable financial planner have discovered that the expense of fees and commissions can be relatively small when compared with the value of the counsel received.

Financial planning services, which used to cater mainly to those of considerable wealth, are now available to millions of people of modest means who lack the time or experience to manage their income and assets properly. The number of financial planners in the United States has increased dramatically since the dawn of the boom years of the 1980s. The National Association of Personal Financial Advisors estimates that between 150,000 and 200,000 people in this country call themselves financial planners.

The Texas State Securities Board, for example, reported that in the first five months of 1996 it received an average of 170 applications to register investment advisor company salespersons each month—a rate more than twice that of previous years. By the end of Illinois's fiscal year ending June 30, 1996, 1,466 investment advisors had been registered by the Securities Department—an increase of 5.7% over the preceding year.

In general, financial planners offer a comprehensive system of money management recommendations, including strategies for investing, cutting taxes, buying insurance, and taking other steps to build income or provide security for the future. Millions of individuals and families have benefited from financial planning services. Others, however, have not only paid good money for bad advice but have gotten badly burned in the process. While most financial planners are honest and reputable, the industry has its fortune hunters whose only objective is to use their customers as stepping-stones to self-enrichment. As in any investment decision, it pays to use care and discrimination when selecting a financial planner.

Variations on a Scheme

For those who fail to check out the honesty and reliability of a prospective financial adviser, it is only too easy to fall into the hands of a professional charlatan. Take the case of James and Laura, a couple of moderate means who could well have benefited from sound financial counseling. As they approached retirement, the pair decided that the savings they had acquired over the years, along with their anticipated pensions, made it advisable to engage the services of a professional financial planner. In fact, they had just received a letter and some printed material in the mail from an investment counseling firm in Chicago, describing its valuable services to people who "with the constant demands on one's time these days, are too busy to manage their money with the care and foresight necessary." The firm would "be happy to evaluate your needs and make an initial recommendation at no cost or commitment to you," the letter promised them.

Deciding that they had nothing to lose and much to gain, James and Laura sent the executive vice president of the company a candid list of their assets, income, and expectations. The response was immediate and enthusiastic, a written proposal that was a bit hard to follow but was filled with glowing promises. In essence, it reported that the couple's net worth was such that they were not even beginning to develop the monetary potential they should already be enjoying. For a very small consulting fee, a mere $1,800, the firm would draw up a financial plan that would help their money make money, quickly covering the modest cost of putting the plan into action.

The $1,800 did indeed seem to be well spent when James and Laura received a personal "evaluation report" and recommendations for "activating" their finances by transferring some of their funds into income-producing investments. It so happened, said the executive VP in a follow-up phone call, that the firm could provide very quick evidence of the kind of prosperity it could generate. The couple only need sell one of their passive assets and place the proceeds, about $5,000, in a little-known but promising high-tech stock venture. The executive VP assured them that there was no risk and that the firm was eager to prove its capabilities to "people like you who will be our blue-chip customers of the future." James and Laura went along with the advice of their newly acquired advisor.

The outcome is easy to guess. The surefire investment was a no-risk one all right—for the bogus financial planning firm. James and Laura never saw a penny of profit and lost all of their initial fee and most of the $5,000. When they tried to track down the executive vice president in his Chicago lair, they discovered that the fancy address was nothing but a tiny back office rented on a monthly basis. They might easily have saved themselves a financial loss, not to mention considerable emotional stress and embarrassment, had they checked out the financial planner in advance.

The following cases illustrate the new type of financial scams by self-proclaimed and registered small investment advisors that state securities enforcement officials are encountering:

- Maryland-based investment advisor Joshua Fry, known widely due to his Saturday-morning radio show, induced his clients to turn over more than $4 million by touting phony performance figures for a bogus mutual fund called the GTC Fund, which stood for "Good 'Til Canceled," that promised "maximum capital growth consistent with the preservation of capital." Fry used the money to run a typical Ponzi scheme in which early investors were paid with later victims' money. The money also supported a lavish lifestyle that included his own horse racing business and gambling junkets. Arrested in Cincinnati, he was ultimately sentenced to eight years in jail.

- In Illinois Howard and John Bozovich were not properly registered as investment advisors. Nevertheless, this father-and-son accounting firm told clients that they would pool their investor funds and purchase various securities. Twelve investors ultimately provided $1.7 million. Investigators from the Illinois Securities Department uncovered massive diversion of investor funds for the personal benefit of the Bozovichs. Victims included an entire church congregation where one of the Bozovichs served as treasurer. Both men were found guilty in state and federal courts. Howard was sentenced to fifteen years, John eleven.

- In Virginia registered investment advisor Robert K. Williams, owner of College Planning Services of Virginia Beach, advertised his expertise in repositioning assets for families seeking financial aid for their college-bound children. Offering fraudulent securities and trust agreements, he obtained $293,000 from fourteen

Virginia investors and used the money to pay for personal and business expenses including a luxury Mercedes with the license plate IPLAN4U. One of his victims was a 19-year-old man who lost $15,000 he had received after his father died from cancer. Williams was convicted on one count of mail fraud, sentenced to 24 months in prison plus three years of probation and ordered to make restitution.

- The Colorado Division of Securities reported that Murleen K. Kunzman swindled $1.8 million from eighty individuals she recruited from her income tax preparation service. In league with her husband and son the Greeley, Colorado woman convinced her carefully selected clients that they would receive returns higher than certificates of deposit from nine separate limited partnerships in residential mortgage loans that she offered. After pleading guilty she was convicted of securities fraud and money laundering and sentenced to fifty-seven months in federal prison. Her former clients lost everything they invested.

- A former pro football player had a history of being disciplined for securities violations by the New York Stock Exchange, the National Association of Securities Dealers, as well as New Hampshire and Vermont, was arrested in September 1995 after a joint investigation by the Vermont Securities Division and the FBI. The accused allegedly ran a Ponzi scheme in which early investors were paid with money provided by later ones, then encouraged to invest even larger sums. Residents of Vermont, New Hampshire, Massachusetts, and Florida may have been bilked out of as much as $30 million. The self-proclaimed investment advisor owned several luxury homes and an airplane, was an avid golfer, and recruited many of his victims from a local country club.

The Facts Behind the Phrase

Just what is a legitimate financial planner? The answer is not all that simple. Many brokers, attorneys, accountants, and insurance agents now promote their services in conjunction with the concept of financial planning. The best of these professionals are knowledgeable about law, accounting, taxation, and insurance, in addition to stocks, bonds, limited partnerships, and other investment subjects. They can advise you regarding ways to structure your estate, lower your taxes, provide for your insurance needs, plan for educating your children, and ensure a comfortable retirement. It is, however, important to realize that, unlike the brokerage industry, the field of financial planning has traditionally been loosely regulated.

Concerned about the nature, number, and varied experience of newcomers in their field, the financial planning trade associations face a double-edged challenge. Some associations want to strengthen actions that would discourage the inept and unethical from doing business. Others want to keep government regulation and restriction at a minimum so that their members can conduct business freely and effectively. All of the trade associations impose some form of standards on members. The International Association for Financial Planning accepts only planners who are willing to abide by its code of ethics and bylaws. The National Association of Personal Financial Advisers limits its membership to fee-only planners, who are compensated through fees but do not derive commissions on investments made for clients. Members of the Institute of Certified Financial Planners (ICFP) must meet standards of education, examination, and experience, and possess the Certified Financial Planner credential.

A private organization affiliated with the ICFP, the Certified Financial Planner Board of Standards certifies individuals as Certified Financial Planners (CFPs). Planners who seek this license must meet certain certification standards, educational requirements, pass an examination, and agree to abide by a code of ethics. More than eighty colleges and universities teach curricula

Preying on the Faithful

A Huntsville, Alabama, man was sentenced to a ten-year prison term after the Alabama Securities Commission found that he took an estimated $18 million from 193 investors in a financial planning scheme that traded on his role as treasurer of the largest Baptist church in the state. The investors, mostly residents of the Huntsville area and members of a particular church, were promised 8 to 30 percent profits per month. "It was sort of comforting," said one victim, "to see the Bible verse printed at the end of the monthly statement."

Securities regulators in several states investigated a Houston, Texas, firm that held financial-planning sessions in communities around the nation. The South Dakota Division of Securities along with other states issued a Cease and Desist Order against the firm. The company's literature announced that its managers were "all Christians" and offered a sort of bargain-basement version of tax evasion through off-shore banking, a scheme that turned out to be fraudulent.

These are only two examples of a sharp increase in the ranks of the "false prophets" of investment—self-proclaimed "born-again" financial planners who claim to be endorsed by local and national church officials and who are only too willing to share "divinely inspired" investment advice. Two-thirds of these schemes are pitched mostly or exclusively to members of one church, with the operators of the swindles appealing to the high level of trust often found in religious groups and communities. In Idaho alone, schemes using religious beliefs to promote investment have amounted to a sobering $27.5 million in losses. While states can and do take action against the violators, it is often too late to recover the money invested.

While some things may be taken on faith, investments are not among them. According to NASAA and the BBB, members of religious communities can protect themselves from

designed to let students qualify for CFP licensing. The course of study generally includes insurance, investments, tax law, and estate planning.

Financial planners may have a variety of other designations and degrees attesting to their education and experience. For example, Chartered Financial Consultants (ChFCs) must complete a correspondence program with eight required courses and two electives, and Chartered Financial Underwriters (CFUs) must complete ten independent self-study courses.

Under the Investment Advisers Act of 1940, financial planners and others who offer, for a fee, to furnish advice on the purchase and sale of securities investment swindles by taking the following common-sense precautions.

1. **Be wary of investments that seem closely tied to a particular religious belief.** It makes little sense that an investment opportunity would be available only to members of a specific church or faith.

2. **Be cautious if the promoter of an investment opportunity tries to capitalize on connections or a leadership position within a religious group.** Remember that the success or failure of any investment is unlikely to be linked to the "inside" contacts of the promoter.

3. **Be on your guard against a new member of church who springs up out of nowhere with a "surefire" investment scheme.** Find out whom you are dealing with and what, if any, that person's background is within the church.

4. **As you would with any investment offer, look closely at investments promoted to you by fellow members of the church.** Friends and fellow believers may unwittingly act as "songbirds" for a swindler's scheme.

5. **Ignore claims that religiously based investments are unregulated.** Virtually *all* investment opportunities, including church bonds, come under the scope of state and federal securities or commodity laws.

6. **Check out the promoter and the investment opportunity.** All promoters—including those who claim church connections—should be checked out thoroughly before money changes hands.

7. **Do not give a break to a swindler who hides behind religion.** Pleas for "Christian forgiveness" are self-serving. Do not be taken advantage of a second time by letting con artists off the hook.

are considered investment advisers and are thus required to register with the Securities and Exchange Commission. In addition, investment advisers must comply with rules that regulate advertising and record keeping and provide disclosure statements to prospective customers. In late October 1996, federal legislation was passed transferring to the states exclusive regulatory authority over investment advisors who manage less than $25 million in assets.

Although investment advisors registering with the SEC are required to file an application that discloses any criminal background, there are no educational or testing requirements for registration. Most states have adopted legislation requiring investment advisors and investment advisor representatives to be licensed on the state level and, in most cases, to meet certain testing requirements. As of October 1996 all states in the United States except Colorado, Wyoming, Iowa, and Ohio regulate investment advisors through their state securities agency. Legislation to regulate investment advisors is expected to be introduced soon in the remaining four states.

NASAA Initiative Protects Investors

In 1996 Congress shifted regulatory oversight of smaller investment advisory firms and financial planners from the SEC to state securities regulators. Under a new two-tier system, investment advisers with more than $25 million in assets under management are required to register with the SEC, while those with less than $25 million in assets must register with the states. In April 1997 state securities officials approved an initiative designed to protect the ever-increasing numbers of consumers who use the services of small investment advisors.

Key elements of the joint-state initiative include:

- Information sharing and communication support among state and provincial securities regulators.
- Consumer awareness programs designed to educate the public about what to look for when choosing a financial planner and what to watch out for in order to avoid fraudulent practices.
- Development of the first exam to ensure a minimum threshold of competency among small advisors throughout the nation.
- Programs to train new regulatory personnel on an annual basis.
- Cooperative operations among states to ensure investment advisor compliance with state laws and regulations designed to protect small investors.
- Development of uniform financial and record-keeping regulations for state-registered advisors.

In addition, the states retain the authority to investigate and bring enforcement actions against SEC-registered advisors in case of fraud or deceit.

Fees and Other Factors

There are basically four categories of financial planners, with each receiving payment in a different way.

- **Fee only.** Fee-only planners charge a fee for developing a financial plan but do not earn income from the financial products they recommend and sell. These planners may charge either a flat fee or an hourly rate. Fees vary widely, but a July 1996 survey of Certified Financial Planners found that the median fee for financial planning services was $100 per hour.

- **Fees and commissions.** Some planners charge a fee for drawing up a financial plan and also receive commissions when you purchase the investments they recommend. Fee-and-commission planners may charge either a flat or an hourly fee for their counsel or they may use a fee scale, with rates dependent on the complexity of the client's financial situation.

- **Commission only.** Commission-only planners charge no fee for their planning services but instead make their money through commissions on the financial products they recommend and sell.

- **Salaried.** These planners work on the staff of a bank, credit union, or other organization offering financial planning services. They typically do not earn fees or commissions, but their employer is compensated through the sale of services and/or investments.

There are advantages and disadvantages to each type of fee arrangement. Your individual financial situation and goals will determine which is best for you. No matter what method of compensation is used, make sure your planner provides you with a written estimate of all fees and commissions.

Getting to Know Your Planner

How can you find a competent, reliable financial planner whose services fit your needs and goals? A good place to start is by surveying friends, relatives, and colleagues who have had satisfactory dealings with their own financial advisors over a period of several years. Keep in mind, though, that a planner who has worked successfully for someone else does not necessarily have experience in the financial areas in which you need help. For additional recommendations, talk to professionals you have worked with in the financial community—brokers, bankers, attorneys, accountants. The professional associations mentioned above and listed in Appendix C also can refer you to planners in your area.

Once you have the names of several prospects, check them out with calls to your state securities division and local Better Business Bureau. Then set up interviews with four or five prospects. Most financial advisors offer a free initial consultation during which you can gather information in the following areas:

- **Education.** Does the advisor have a degree in financial planning or a related field and/or hold one or more credentials such as CFP, ChFC, CLU, CPA (Certified Public Accountant), or CPA/PFS (Certified Public Accountant/Personal Financial Specialist)? Ask for an explanation of the requirements for use of the title, and verify credentials with the associations listed in Appendix C.

- **Affiliation.** What professional and/or trade associations does the planner belong to? Membership in an industry group is no guarantee of competence or integrity, but it may indicate that the planner has met certain standards and requirements. Be sure to verify what you are told with a phone call to the organization.

- **Experience.** How long has the advisor been practicing financial planning and what did the advisor do before becoming a financial planner? In general, you should look for three or more years of experience as a financial planner and several additional years of prior experience as a broker, insurance agent, accountant, or lawyer.

- **Expertise.** What are the advisor's areas of expertise or practice specialty? Financial professionals may specialize in one or more areas of financial planning or in certain types of client. Compare their expertise to your needs and goals. Also ask whether you can expect referrals to other sources of assistance if the need arises for services outside the planner's areas of expertise.

- **Method of operation.** Find out if the planner will be turning over all or most of the day-to-day handling of your financial plan to associates. If so, take the time to check out those individuals too. Also ask to see examples of plans and monitoring reports drawn up for other clients. Pay particular attention to the frequency and quality of the monitoring reports, as these will be vital to reviewing and recharting your financial plan.

- **Reputation.** Will the advisor provide references from other professionals and from three or more clients? Do not hesitate to call these references to ask about their experiences and affiliation with the planner.

- **Registration and licensing.** What products is the advisor licensed to sell, if any? Are the licenses current? Is the advisor registered/licensed with your state securities regulator or the SEC as a Registered Investment Advisor?

If you feel that the procedure is all too complicated and involved, take heart from the case of former teacher Rickie Cowin, who, at the age of thirty-five, took her small savings and went into real estate. Admitting that her financial knowledge "bordered on the nonexistent," she located a reliable financial advisor who charged no advance fee but worked on a commission basis. The planner placed about $6,000 of her funds in a short-term certificate of deposit as a starter, helping her to read and understand the bank statements when they arrived in the mail. Even this small financial move was a traumatic experience for Rickie. "I'm very conservative," she said. "I would sleep with my money in my hands if I could."

As her income grew and the CD matured, she accepted the planner's advice to invest in public utilities. "We always need gas and electricity," she assured herself, trying to overcome innate doubts about venturing over her head in the investment sea.

Over a six-year period, Cowin came to trust her planner's advice, as well as to have more confidence in her own decision making. After realizing a 160 percent return on her utility stocks and discussing ways of broadening her investment plan, she closed what was left of her savings account in favor of a cash management account. "Saying good-bye to the bank was a big deal for me," she admitted, confirming that her attitude had changed greatly as a result of establishing and meeting realistic financial goals.

Financial planning is not for everyone. And putting yourself in the hands of an inept or unethical financial planner is worse than having no plan at all. But it makes sense to undertake a serious study of what can be done with your assets both to make profits and to ensure a more secure future. If you study your options and investigate thoroughly before making any commitments, you are almost certain to come out ahead of the game.

What to Expect/What to Avoid

Here are some additional pointers from NASAA and the BBB on what services you should expect from a financial planner along with precautions that should alert you to possible misrepresentation or fraud.

Your financial planner should provide:

- A clearly written plan, in language you can understand, containing a balance sheet of profits versus liabilities, a projected cash flow statement, and a definition of your financial goals and the steps you will take to achieve them.
- Disclosure of the amount of risk estimated in pursuit of the objectives.
- Disclosure of commissions or other incentives the planner will receive from recommended investment vehicles.
- Specific suggestions for improving your personal cash management.
- Projections for shifts in interest rates, inflation, tax laws, and other conditions that might affect your plan in the future.

- Options and alternatives providing a range of investment choices, with a list of the advantages and disadvantages of each.
- A plan for liquidity in the event of emergency, outlining ways to obtain reserve cash with the least amount of disruption and cost.
- Suggested sources of tax or legal services from other professionals, such as accountants, attorneys, insurance agents, or stockbrokers.
- A proposed schedule for implementing and monitoring your financial plan and periodically reviewing its progress and objectives.

Be wary of:

- Oversimplified, computer-generated plans that do not fit your individual financial needs.
- Plans that give you few or no investment alternatives.
- High-pressure tactics or promises of unrealistically high profits or "no-risk" investments.
- Recommendations for ventures whose purpose is unstated or unclear, or for exotic-sounding ventures such as rare coins or ultrahigh-tech developments.
- Claims that an investment strategy is so complicated only the financially astute can understand it.

Guidelines for a Sound Financial Plan

Before you can expect a competent planner to help you make financial decisions, you must have a clear picture of your current financial profile, needs, and goals. The following steps are a necessary part of the financial planning process:

1. Compile all the data you can—the more specific the better—concerning your income, bank accounts, real estate holdings, income taxes, wills, loans, budget, and related financial matters. Organize all important papers and financial documents.
2. Identify your short- and long-term goals, whether as an individual, a couple, or a family. Decide what financial risks you are willing to take in pursuit of your goals.
3. List any major anticipated changes that could modify your objectives. These might include marriage, children, retirement, change of job, or relocation.
4. Figure out your assets and liabilities—what you own and what you owe. Identify financial crises and trouble spots such as mounting debts, tax increases, or chronic illness.
5. Make a list of other professionals who currently assist you or have in the past, including attorneys, accountants, brokers, and bankers.

Chapter 12

How To Select and Work With A Stockbroker

After her late husband's estate had been settled and the life insurance paid, a widow found herself with $200,000 in the bank. Relatives urged her to invest in securities so that she could live on the proceeds and not have to dip into capital.

After listening to suggestions from friends who had been in similar circumstances, the woman visited the offices of a local stockbroker for guidance. The broker helped her put a sound financial program in place, with a healthy balance of growth and income investments. It was reassuring to be in the hands of a financial expert who seemed both reputable and professional. In fact, when the broker decided to move to another firm, the widow agreed to transfer her entire account to the new firm. That is when her troubles began.

Adhering to industry policy, the broker completed a new-account form. But in filling it out, he altered the widow's designated investment objectives, without her knowledge or consent, in a way that gave his firm approval for trading in all kinds of options. The woman had orally authorized the broker to exercise discretion with her account as long as he acted in accordance with her conservative investment objectives. Instead, the broker went on what one securities regulator described as a "commission-generating rampage," completing more than 170 trades in the course of a single year.

While the broker realized commissions of almost $70,000, the net loss to his customer's account was close to $35,000. It was a classic case of "churning"—excessive trading by a broker to make more in commissions while disregarding the best interests of the client. The widow, disillusioned and disgusted, brought legal action against the broker and his firm. She received a $54,000 settlement and had the satisfaction of seeing the broker barred from industry membership.

The vast majority of investment professionals are never accused of fraud or abuse. However, there *are* brokers who engage in misconduct. Even the most honest and conscientious broker may be unable to meet your expectations 100 percent and may even make decisions that negatively affect the value of your portfolio. Still, there is much you can do to increase your chances of establishing a good relationship with your stockbroker and realizing your investment goals. The key is knowledge: knowing yourself, knowing the broker, and knowing the investment alternatives.

Establishing Goals

About 52 million investors in the United States own stock in companies or shares in stock mutual funds. Most of these people—including experienced investors who are confident about choosing investments themselves and those with less experience who need expert advice on how and where to invest—work with a stockbroker at some point. A stockbroker ("broker"), also known as a registered representative or account executive, is a financial professional who works for a company called a broker-dealer of securities, or brokerage firm. Broker-dealers and their account executives make money through commissions on the securities bought and sold by their clients.

The first step in selecting a brokerage firm and an individual broker is to determine your personal financial needs and investment objectives. Are you seeking long-term growth, a steady income flow, tax savings, quick profits, or a combination of these? If you enjoy a good household income, are relatively young, and can handle a degree of risk in order to seek larger gains down the road, your goal might well be growth through the appreciation of capital. If you are living on a fixed income, your objective may be to protect your capital while bringing in a more modest income through dividends and interest.

Check the data and figures in your personal financial analysis with an accountant or another professional familiar with your financial status. For help in drawing up a long-term financial plan, you may want to consult a financial planner (see chapter 11, "How to Select and Work With a Financial Planner"). If you are married, your spouse should share in the evaluation and planning. If there is a financial interdependence between you and your parents, adult children, or other close relatives, you might make those persons a party to your financial planning.

Once you have made an honest and realistic appraisal of your financial situation and investment goals, you are ready to seek out the stockbroker who will best serve your interests.

Selecting and Checking Out a Broker

Stockbrokers fall into two basic categories—full-service and discount. There are advantages and disadvantages to working with each.

The full-service broker researches and recommends particular investments tailored to your financial situation. If you do not fully understand an investment, a full-service broker can explain it. Working with this type of broker gives you the advantage of having a professional to whom you can turn for both services and

Crackdown Aimed at Stockbrokers Who Fleece Investors Over the Telephone

On May 29, 1997 NASAA announced that twenty state securities agencies filed thirty-six actions against fourteen firms in the biggest nationwide crackdown ever by the states aimed at brokers selling stocks over the phone.

"Reading from scripts, employees of these firms pressure(d) their victims to buy stock in unknown companies," said NASAA President Mark J. Griffin. "Once the price is driven high enough, insiders sell the stock making fortunes for themselves and wiping out the savings of innocent investors."

The origins of the crackdown go back to the late fall of 1996 when NASAA's board of directors authorized a special project to address the problem of fraudulent sales practices in the micro-cap marketplace. In January 1997 a strike force comprised of representatives from twelve states was created and divided into teams, each targeting a particular firm. In addition branch offices and additional firms in other dates were also scheduled for audits. Then in late February the teams struck without warning. State examiners discovered four systemic abuses:

- Abusive cold calling practices. Most of the firms and branches relied on high-pressure, scripted telephone cold calling techniques that include falsifying experience and performance as well as other outright lies.

- Sales practice abuses. Examiners found an army of unlicensed solicitors who are accused of falsifying records, conducting unauthorized trades, and failing to complete trades.

- Failure to report investor complaints. State examiners found hundreds unreported. Most of the offices audited failed to have centralized procedures for handling and reporting customer complaints.

- Evasion of broker-dealer registration requirements through use of third party franchise agreements.

"Historically when you shine a light on these types of firms, the individuals who organize and participate in them disperse like cockroaches running for cover, only to turn up later. But for these of you who engage in these types of practices let me tell you, we're going to track you down wherever you go and put you out of business," warned NASAA.

The twenty states participating in this special project included: Alabama, Connecticut, Delaware, Illinois, Indiana, Maryland, Massachusetts, Missouri, New Hampshire, New Jersey, New Mexico, New York, Ohio, Oklahoma, Pennsylvania, Texas, Utah, Vermont, Washington, and Wisconsin.

Beware of Risky Investment Sales: Derivatives

The Wisconsin securities administrator suspended a securities agent's license (in action timed so that the agent is in fact now out of business) for conduct in placing unsophisticated investors into "derivatives" investments often in unauthorized trades. "Derivatives" are complicated and extremely risky positions in various products in which two or more parties contractually agree upon some payment based on (or "derived" from) a benchmark. The agent did not explain the instruments or the great risks in investing in them to his customers.

Understanding such instruments fully and their risks requires extreme financial sophistication and even knowledge of advanced mathematics. Ordinarily only knowledgeable investors should ever invest in such instruments; even they sometimes get fooled with respect to "derivatives." And even some financial institutions have alleged that they have been defrauded in their purchases of these kinds of securities. Such "derivatives" were the downfall of an Orange County [California] investment officer in a highly publicized case two years ago.

Wisconsin has noticed that investors sometimes see such instruments appearing in their brokerage accounts but do not realize what they are because their descriptions sometimes make them appear to the unknowledgeable as simply some sort of U.S. government issued or guaranteed notes. Investors generally should stay away from investing in such instruments, and if they see references to what look like government or government-agency bonds or notes in their brokerage statements and are not intimately familiar with them, they should demand a detailed explanation from their brokerage firm or even from their state securities administrator.

advice. Full-service brokers charge commissions for buying or selling securities. Commission rates vary from firm to firm and also from client to client within the firm, depending on factors such as the size of transactions, the volume of business done by the customer, and the services performed.

Discount brokers place orders to buy or sell securities at your request; they generally do not recommend specific securities or investment strategies. If you understand the market, do all your own investment research, and need a broker only to execute transactions, you might consider using a discount brokerage firm. Discount brokers generally charge a considerably lower commission rate than full-service brokers.

Once you have decided which type of service you will require from a broker, you are ready to begin your search. Brokerage relationships are highly personal, and your satisfaction will depend not only on the firm but also on the account executive you select. Many people ask for recommendations from friends, business associates, or professionals they know and trust. It may be helpful to speak with people who have financial circumstances and objectives similar to your own. Keep in mind, though, that a recommendation is no guarantee that what is right for one individual will also be right for you.

Check out prospective firms by phoning or meeting with local branch office managers. Ask about and compare services and training programs. Find out if the firm is a member of the National Association of Securities Dealers (NASD) and the Securities Investor Protection Corporation (SIPC) (see Appendix C). NASD is a self-regulatory broker-dealer organization that imposes standards of fair practice on its members and takes disciplinary action against members who violate its rules. SIPC is an organization that protects investors who have money or securities in a brokerage account if the broker-dealer ceases business or goes bankrupt. SIPC does not protect against losses due to a decline in the market value of securities. Phone your local Better Business Bureau (see Appendix A) to find out if there have been investor complaints against the brokerage firm or the individual broker. Also ask your state securities agency (see Appendix B) for answers to the following questions:

- Is the firm licensed/registered to sell securities in your state?
- Is the broker licensed/registered to sell securities in your state?
- Is there a history of regulatory violations, disciplinary actions, or investor complaints involving the broker or firm?

Your state securities agency also can provide a copy of the firm's and the broker's Central Registration Depository report (see "CRD Reports," below).

Now, at last, you are ready to schedule face-to-face interviews with prospective brokers. Look for someone who listens to your concerns and answers your questions fully. You should feel comfortable enough to share very personal information about your financial means and goals. You will also want to look for a broker who explains things until you understand them and does not pressure you into acting. Ask about the broker's training, education, and experience, and remember that you will need someone who is both knowledgeable and willing to take the time to find the investment strategy that is best for you.

Ask whether the broker or firm specializes in mutual funds, government bonds, municipal bonds, tax shelters, or other products. Also ask to see samples of account statements. Some firms issue statements with sketchy and confusing information, while others go to great pains to make their periodic statements more readable and informative. Request a full explanation of commission rates. What services are provided free and what services do you pay for? Armed with all this information, only you can judge whether a firm's and broker's services, commission structure, and "personality" are compatible with your objectives.

Informed and in Charge

Once you select a broker, you will be asked a series of questions needed to fill out the required new-account form. Among other things, your broker may ask about your income and assets, career and retirement plans, investment

CRD Reports

A Central Registration Depository (CRD) report is actually a compilation of reports, stored in a computer database, containing information on the employment and disciplinary history of all brokers and other financial advisers. Brokers should be able to give you their CRD number. Using that identification number, your state securities agency can search the database for a broker's report.

CRD reports contain information about a broker's employment history along with other information. However, if complaints or actions have been filed against a broker, the report also will include details such as a description of the problem or allegation, the broker's explanation of the incident, and any disciplinary actions taken. The codes and the presentation of facts in a CRD that includes disciplinary information can be somewhat difficult to decipher. If there is any-thing you do not understand, you can contact the agency that sent you the report for an explanation.

Your decision on whether or not to select a particular broker should not be based solely on the CRD file. However, CRD information can be an important part of your decision making. If you are leaning toward a particular broker because of satisfactory interviews and other investigations, a report showing that the broker has been in business for a good number of years without complaints or disciplinary action should make you feel more comfortable about your decision. On the other hand, you may find so much negative or disturbing information about a broker that you decide to continue your search elsewhere. Before making that decision, be sure to review the CRD report carefully to get a clear understanding of the final disposition of the complaints, charges, or arbitration filings.

objectives, and the degree of risk you are willing and able to take in investing. Do not take offense at any questions that seem to pry into your personal affairs. Your broker's advice can only be as good as the information on which it is based. In fact, if you decide any of the broker's questions are too personal to answer, the firm has the right to refuse to open your account.

Be sure to read your new-account form and any other agreements carefully before signing. Additional forms may be required if you desire certain services, such as buying on margin (purchasing securities with money borrowed from the brokerage firm at interest) or opening a discretionary account, which gives the broker the right to buy and sell securities for you without receiving specific approval for each transaction. Make sure all the lines on all forms are filled in or crossed out, and never sign a blank form. Be sure to get a copy of all agreements for your records.

The fact that you have selected a broker in whom you have confidence does not mean you can turn your back on your investments and let the account representative handle the details. A wise investor is an informed investor, one who studies the market regularly and can ask intelligent questions about various securities. This is increasingly important in light of the many complex financial instruments being offered today. Read the business section of your newspaper and check the Internet and your local library or bookstore for current financial guides. If you own stock in publicly held corporations, read their annual reports and quarterly or other periodic statements. You might consider subscribing to a business periodical or to investment newsletters specializing in your areas of interest. Take the time to read the newsletters and other publications that are mailed to you by the brokerage firm or that can be obtained on request from the firm's research department. Many firms also have toll-free numbers you can phone for daily updates on stock and mutual fund prices and your portfolio value.

Keep track of what is happening in your account by reading your periodic statements and the written confirmation that you should receive after every transaction. Make certain those documents accurately reflect what has happened in your account and that what happened was what you *wanted* to happen. If you do not understand statements or confirmations, ask the account executive to explain them.

It is important to keep good records in case securities are lost or stolen. The Securities and Exchange Commission recommends that investors keep a record of all transactions in a book or file separate from the actual securities certificates. These records should include the cost of securities, the name of

Overseeing Your Investments

Whether you are working with a broker or any other investment professional, it is crucial to stay actively involved in the management of your account. The following steps can help investors avoid problems by taking charge of their money.

1. **Map out your financial goals before meeting with a financial planner, stockbroker, investment adviser, or other investment professional.** The experts may be able to help you decide how to invest your funds, but you must first have a firm grasp of your short- and long-term goals and needs. How much income do you need to meet fixed expenses? Do you have children or grandchildren to educate? Are your parents in need of eldercare? How is your own health? Determine your budget needs and your ability to tolerate risk first, *then* decide what kinds of investments will best fulfill those goals.

2. **Know your investment professional.** Always take time to interview two or three investment professionals before settling on the one who seems best suited to your needs. Check out all prospects with a call to your local Better Business Bureau and state securities agency. Remember, however, that a license is not a guarantee of good performance. It does give state securities agencies the opportunity to review a person's background before allowing that person to sell securities to the public.

3. **Understand your investment.** Before purchasing any investment, you should understand the cost, the degree and nature of the risks, the investment goals, the performance history, and any special fees associated with the investment. Never assume that an investment is federally insured, low-risk, or guaranteed to deliver a certain return. And do not rely on verbal statements about an investment. Get them in writing, and make sure you understand the information you are given. In most

the brokerage firm where they were purchased, and the certificate number(s) for all certificates received. You also will need these records to determine a security's gains or losses for income tax purposes when the security is sold.

If Something Goes Wrong

Where can you turn if you have problems with your account or your broker? First, you must determine where the fault lies. Some investors simply expect too much, as though brokers possessed hidden powers of insight that was instances, you do not have the right to cancel a transaction after it has been made.

4. **Understand how your financial professional is making money by selling an investment.** Keep in mind that brokers and some financial planners make commissions when you buy or sell recommended investments. Do not confuse a sales pitch with impartial advice that takes into account your individual goals, risk tolerance, and current assets. Also be wary of investment professionals who seem overly eager to put you into exotic investments or an in-house fund. Ask if the broker receives an extra commission or other incentives for selling the financial product.

5. **Know the product you are buying when purchasing on the premises of a bank.** Although a bank may provide you with more convenience and be less intimidating than a brokerage firm, it does not offer any more assurance against the possible loss of principal in an uninsured investment. Don't let convenience guide your decision about where to invest.

6. **Make sure you fully understand your account statements.** Account statements are your primary tool for policing your investments, so take full advantage of them. Statements should reflect only the pattern of investing that you have authorized. If you spot possible problems, take immediate steps to resolve them. Also review your statements with an eye to how your investments are performing and how much they are costing you in terms of commissions and fees. Your financial professional can help you calculate these figures and can provide the results in writing. Do not work with someone who is unwilling or claims to be unable to provide this information.

7. **Never be afraid to ask questions at any stage of the investment process.** If you are uncertain about investment advice, ask questions until you understand. Even if you hire an expert to help manage your money, *you* are the person in control and you have every right to understand what is happening with your investments.

theirs alone. Clairvoyance in the investment field exists mainly in hindsight; it is all too easy to decide after the fact what should have been done. Other investors run into problems because they have not presented their needs and goals clearly or have indulged in wishful thinking when imparting their financial objectives to their brokers.

Real problems can arise, however, even when the initial communication has been clear and the goals mutually understood. Some of these problems are functional, such as the late delivery of a stock certificate or dividend check. Other problems may be more serious, involving sales practices that have weakened your control of the account and muddled its objectives.

One of the most common and troubling abuses, discussed earlier, is churning—excessive trading by a broker to generate commissions. Other types of investment fraud and abuse include:

- **Unsuitable investments**—the recommendation of investments that are not appropriate to a particular investor's financial situation, needs, and objectives.
- **Unauthorized trading**—transactions carried out without a client's prior permission (illegal except in accounts where discretion has been given in writing to the account executive).
- **Misrepresentations/omissions**—untruthful or incomplete representations of investment opportunities.
- **Theft**—outright theft of client funds.

Whenever you suspect there may be a problem with the way your investments have been handled, take steps to resolve it immediately. State laws limit the amount of time you have in which to take action against a broker; if you let that time elapse, it might become impossible to recover your losses. Brokerage firms are more willing to cancel trades or adjust accounts if problems are brought to their attention immediately, before any losses occur.

Your first step should be to contact your account representative. Spell out the problem and the resolution you expect within a specific period of time. Always follow up telephone complaints with a formal letter to confirm the points discussed.

If you are told that the broker is away, ill, on vacation, or otherwise unavailable, or if the situation is not corrected within the specified time, contact the firm's branch office manager. Have available all recent statements from the firm so that you can verify or question any transactions about which you have doubts. Again, put your complaint in writing.

What if you speak to both your broker and the office manager and still are unable to resolve the problem? Your next recourse is to contact the chief compliance officer at the firm's home office, whose name must be given to you on request. Send a copy of your correspondence to your state securities agency. If you still do not get a satisfactory response, contact your state securities agency, the self-regulatory organizations to which the firm belongs, and your local Better Business Bureau.

If all else fails and you still believe that you have lost investment money as a result of broker misconduct, you may wish to consider arbitration or legal action. Nearly all brokerage firms now require customers to agree to arbitration instead of proceeding to court. Arbitration is a method of resolving a dispute between two parties through the intervention of an impartial third party knowledgeable in the area of controversy. This offers a less costly and generally faster means of settlement than conventional litigation. It is vital to understand, however, that arbitration awards are final. By agreeing to arbitration as a means of resolving a dispute, you forgo your right to pursue the matter through the courts should the decision go against you. If you are unfamiliar with securities laws and the process of arbitration, you may choose to hire an attorney to represent you in the arbitration process.

Chances are good that if you follow the suggestions outlined earlier, you will never be in the position of having to seek arbitration to resolve a dispute with your brokerage firm or account representative. Be an informed and aware investor, alert to changes in the market and the economic trends that shape the course of the money world. Never hesitate to ask tough questions of anyone who has or is seeking access to your funds, and do not be embarrassed to say "no" to any recommendation you believe is off target. Bear in mind that there is risk in any investment, and that the greater the profit potential, the greater the risk.

And no matter whom you are dealing with—a stockbroker, a financial planner, or any company or individual who has contacted you by phone, mail, or e-mail—remember, ***if an offer sounds too good to be true, it probably is.***

Annual report. A formal statement issued yearly by a corporation to its shareholders, showing assets, liabilities, equity, revenues, and expenses, and reflecting the corporation's status at the close of the business year.

Antifraud provisions. Federal and state securities law provisions imposing liability for, among other things, omission or misstatement of fact in the sale or purchase of securities.

Application mill. A fraudulent company that offers its services to help consumers invest in FCC licenses for providing telecommunications services in a specific market. Application mills typically mislead investors about the costs and potential profits and risks of investing in licenses.

Arbitration. A system for resolving disputes in which all parties submit their disagreement to an impartial panel for resolution. Decisions of an arbitration panel are binding on the parties to the claim.

Ask price. The lowest price a broker asks customers to pay for a security at a given time.

Assets. Everything of value that a company or individual owns or has due.

Bid price. The highest price a broker is willing to pay for a security at a given time.

Blind pools. Investments in companies about which investors are provided with little or no meaningful information. Blank-check blind pools often are sham corporations, usually with no assets, employees, or stated business plan, used as vehicles for stock price manipulation.

Blue chip. Common stock in a company nationally known for the quality and wide acceptance of its products and services and for its ability to make money and pay dividends.

Boiler room. A temporary office equipped with phones from which con artists call lists of prospects to talk them into purchasing worthless or greatly overpriced securities or other investments.

Bond. A certificate that is evidence of a debt in which the issuer promises to repay a specific amount of money to the bond holder, plus a certain amount of interest, within a fixed period of time.

Broker. An agent or account executive who works for a broker-dealer and earns commissions on the sale or purchase of securities on behalf of clients.

Broker-dealer. A firm engaged in the business of buying or selling securities for its own account or for clients; commonly called a "brokerage firm."

Bucket shop. An operation similar to a boiler room, except that boiler-room operators typically peddle actual investments of little or no value, while bucket-shop operators take victims' money without ever buying or selling the securities or other investments the client orders.

Call options/provisions. A transaction in which an investor sells or buys the right to buy a specific security at a specific price within a fixed period of time. Also refers to provisions in bond contracts that allow issuers to buy back bonds prior to their stated maturity.

Cash forward account. An often fraudulent form of commodities instrument that is not traded through regulated commodities exchanges.

Certified Financial Planner (CFP). A financial planner who becomes qualified to use the title of CFP after meeting requirements based on education and experience.

Churning. Excessive trading of a customer's account by a broker who has control over trading decisions and whose sole purpose is to generate commissions.

Commission. The fee charged by a broker-dealer for buying or selling securities on behalf of a client.

Commission-only planner. A financial planner who does not charge a fee for developing a financial plan but earns commissions on the sale or purchase of the investments recommended.

Commodity. An article of commerce in which contracts for future delivery may be traded. Common commodities include corn, cotton, livestock, copper, gold, silver, petroleum, currency, Treasury bills, and bonds.

CRD (Central Registration Depository) Report. A computer database compilation of reports on the employment and disciplinary history of brokers and other financial advisors, available through state securities administrators and the National Association of Securities Dealers.

Cyberschemes. Fraudulent investment schemes perpetrated through computer bulletin boards, chat rooms, unsolicited e-mails, and web sites on the Internet.

Deferred delivery contract. An often fraudulent form of commodity instrument that is not traded through regulated exchanges. The contract involves the purchase or sale of commodities or securities to be delivered at a specified future date; also called "delayed delivery contract."

Discount broker. A broker who places orders to buy or sell securities on behalf of clients but does not research and recommend specific investments.

Discretionary account. A type of account with a broker-dealer in which the investor authorizes the broker to buy and sell securities selected by the broker, without obtaining specific prior approval for each transaction.

Dividend. A payment by a corporation to its stockholders, usually representing a share in the company's earnings.

Face value. The redemption value of a bond or preferred stock, appearing on the face of the certificate; also called "par value."

FDIC (Federal Deposit Insurance Corporation). An agency of the federal government created to guarantee bank deposits.

Fee-and-commission planner. A financial planner who charges a fee for developing a financial plan and also earns commissions on the sale or purchase of recommended investments.

Fee-only planner. A financial planner who charges a fee for developing a financial plan but does not earn income from the sale or purchase of the financial products recommended.

Fee-simple agreement. A type of time-share agreement in which investors each have an ownership interest in the time-share property; also called a "deeded" agreement.

Financial planner. An individual who provides clients with a personalized financial plan that may include strategies for investing, cutting taxes, buying insurance, building income, and providing security for the future.

Forward contract. A transaction in which the buyer and seller of a commodity agree upon delivery of a specified quantity and quality of the commodity at a specified future date.

Franchise. An agreement through which an individual or a group purchases the right to market products or services under the name of the corporation selling the franchise.

Full-service broker. A broker who researches and recommends investments tailored to the financial profile of specific clients and also buys and sells securities on behalf of clients.

Futures contract. A commitment to receive or deliver a specified quantity and grade of a commodity during a designated period of time, with the price determined by public auction among exchange members.

Infomercial. A program-length television or radio commercial.

Interactive video and data service (IVDS). A small portion of the radio spectrum set aside by the FCC to allow users to send limited data responses to interactive TV programming. This legitimate technology often is exploited by fraudulent application mills.

Investment company. A company engaged primarily in the business of investing in securities.

"IRA-approved" investment schemes. Schemes in which promoters induce victims to transfer their retirement funds to high-risk or fraudulent investment accounts, often by stating or implying that the federal government has approved or endorsed the proposed investments.

Issue. A series or class of securities that has been or is being sold by a company. Also refers to the marketing and distributing of a new class or type of securities.

Junk bonds. High-yield, high-risk, low-rated or nonrated bonds, often associated with corporate takeovers.

Leverage contract. A standardized agreement calling for delivery of a commodity, with payments against the total cost spread out over a term of years; also called "margin account" or "leverage account."

Limited partnership. A legal entity consisting of one or more general partners and a larger number of limited partners. As a general rule, the general partners provide management of the underlying business and the limited partners provide the capital for business operations.

Manipulation. The illegal practice of buying or selling securities for the purpose of creating a false appearance of active trading, thus raising or depressing the price to induce purchases or sales by others.

Margin account. A type of account with a broker-dealer in which the firm agrees to lend the customer part of the amount due for the purchase of securities.

Margin deposit. The amount of money or other collateral deposited to insure a broker against loss on futures contracts; also called "initial margin."

Market value. The price at which an investor could buy or sell a bond or other security, as opposed to its face value.

Maturity. The value on which a loan, bond, or debenture comes due.

Misappropriation. The unauthorized use of or interference with the right of ownership over money, investments, or property.

Misrepresentation. False or misleading statements made to a customer in order to influence decisions involving purchases or investments.

Multilevel marketing. A method for selling products or services in which participants act as independent distributors, earning income from their own sales and from sales made by other distributors whom they have recruited and trained. Pyramid schemes often are disguised as legitimate multilevel marketing opportunities.

New issue stocks. A new offering of securities by a company seeking public financing for the first time, in which the price is expected to rise to a substantial premium over the initial offering price either immediately or very soon after the securities are first offered to the public. Often promoted as a "sure thing," new issues are a high-risk investment in which prices fluctuate widely.

Nondisclosure. Failure to disclose key facts needed by a customer to make decisions about trading in securities or other investments.

Option. A trading tool used in commerce that gives the buyer the right to buy or sell a quantity of a commodity or security at a specific pre-arranged price within a specified time period, regardless of the market price of the commodity or security at that time.

Over-the-counter market. A market in which securities not listed on a national exchange are traded, mainly over the telephone.

Penny stocks. Low-priced securities, usually traded at under $5 per share in the over-the-counter market, issued for the most part by companies with little business experience.

Pink sheets. A daily published listing of prices of over-the-counter stocks, including some penny stocks (so named for the color of the paper on which it is printed).

Ponzi scheme. One of the oldest and simplest forms of investment swindles, in which victims' money is never invested in anything. Early investors are paid "gains" out of money put up by later investors.

Portfolio. The list of securities held by an individual or institution, or the commercial paper held by a bank or other financial house.

Prime bank guarantees. Questionable financial instruments that promoters claim are guaranteed by well-known foreign financial institutions; also called "prime bank notes," "prime bank letters of credit," "prime European bank letters of credit," "prime world bank debentures," and "prime insurance guarantees."

Promoter. An individual or firm that directly or indirectly takes the initiative in trying to induce investors to put money into an enterprise or to purchase securities or other investments.

Prospectus. A document required by law to be furnished to purchasers of securities; it provides detailed information about the company issuing the securities and about the specific offering.

Pump and dump. An on-line investment scheme in which promoters post numerous bulletin board messages under different screen names, calculated to spark interest in a little-known, thinly traded stock so that the price will rise and promoters can sell their shares at a profit.

Pyramid scheme. An illegal scheme in which investors are sold the right to become a sales representative or member, with the right to sell the same privilege to others. The sale of a product may be involved but is always secondary to the recruitment of new participants.

Recovery rooms. Schemes in which victims of previous investment schemes are targeted a second time by the same or another promoter offering, for a fee, to recover lost funds; also called "reload scams" or "double-scams."

Registered securities. Stocks, bonds, or other securities for which a registration statement has been filed with state securities administrators and the SEC.

Reparations award. The amount of monetary damages a party has been ordered by law to pay.

Repurchase agreement. An agreement by the seller of a security to later repurchase the security by repaying the buyer's purchase price plus interest; also called "repo."

Right-to-use agreement. A type of time-share agreement in which investors do not have an ownership interest in the time-share property but are entitled to use the property for specified periods of time for a specified number of years; also called a "non-deeded" or "lease" agreement.

Security. A stock, bond, note, investment contract, or similar instrument.

Service fee. A fee charged in lieu of commissions for services rendered.

Settlement group. A group of investors who are seeking an

FCC license for providing telecommunications services in a given market and who agree to join together and share the interest in a license; also called an "alliance."

Specialized mobile radio (SMR). A set of dedicated radio frequencies or channels allocated by the FCC primarily to transmit and receive paging, data communications, and voice transmission. This legitimate technology often is exploited by fraudulent application mills.

Spread. The difference between a security's bid and ask price quotations.

Stock. An ownership interest in a company; also called "shares" in a company.

Sucker lists. Lists of victims compiled, traded, and sold by fraudulent telemarketers.

Telemarketing. The marketing of goods and services by phone. This legitimate business is often exploited by boiler-room operators.

Telemarketing Sales Rule. Legislation enacted by the Federal Trade Commission in 1995 that requires telemarketers to provide specified information to prospects to enable them to make informed buying decisions.

Time-sharing. An investment in which individuals share in the ownership or rental of a property that each uses on a part-time, rotating basis.

Unauthorized trading. Purchase or sale of securities or other investments for a client by a broker without the client's permission.

Voice-switching. A technique used by boiler-room operators in which a salesperson's pitch to a prospect is interrupted by another con artist claiming to be an officer of the company with exciting new information compelling an immediate investment.

Wireless cable television. A technology that uses microwaves to relay cable television programs to rooftop antennas at the homes of subscribers. This legitimate high-tech industry often is exploited by fraudulent application mills.

Yield. The return on an investment in a stock or bond, calculated as a percentage of the amount invested.

Zero coupon bonds. Bonds that can be purchased at a fraction of their future value at maturity, sometimes at just a few pennies on the dollar. Zeros are so named because they pay no periodic coupon payments.

APPENDIX A

The Council of Better Business Bureaus (CBBB) is the umbrella organization for 135 Better Business Bureaus (BBBs) across the U.S. Through the national memberships of more than 350 leading edge companies and the network of member BBBs, the Council promotes the highest ethical relationship between businesses and the public through voluntary self-regulation, consumer and business education, and service excellence.

Council of Better Business Bureaus, INC.

4200 Wilson Blvd.
Arlington, VA 22203
(703) 276-0100 Fax (703) 525-8277
World Wide Web: http://www.bbb.org

United States Bureaus (BBBs)

ALABAMA

Birmingham, AL 35205
1210 S. 20th St.
P.O. Box 55268 (35255)
(205) 558-2222

Cullman, AL 35057
1528 Peachtree Ln., Suite 1
(205) 772-2917
No. AL only
(800) 239-1642

Dothan, AL 36301
118 Woodburn
(334) 794-0492

Florence, AL 35630
121 A South Court St.
No. AL only (800) 239-1642 (24hrs)

Huntsville, AL 35801-5549
107 Lincoln St., NE
P.O. Box 383 (35804)
(205) 533-1640

Mobile, AL 36602-3295
100 N. Royal St.
(334) 433-5494
So. Al (800) 544-4714

Montgomery, AL 36104-3559
60 Commerce St., Suite 806
(334) 262-5606

ALASKA

Anchorage, AK 99503-3819
2805 Bering Street, Suite 5
(907) 562-0704

Fairbanks, AK 99707
P.O. Box 74675
(907) 451-0222

Kenai, AK 99611
P.O. Box 1229
(907) 283-4880

ARIZONA

Phoenix, AZ 85014-4585
4428 North 12th St.
($3.80/all)
CC# (602) 240-3973
(95¢/min., 24 hrs.)
(900) 225-5222

Tucson, AZ 85719
3620 N. 1st Ave., Ste. 136
Inq. (520) 888-5353
Comp. (520) 888-5454
So. AZ (800) 696-2827

ARKANSAS

Little Rock, AR 72204-2605
1415 South University
(501) 664-7274
AR only (800) 482-8448

CALIFORNIA

**Bakersfield, CA
93301-4882**
705 18th St.
(805) 322-2074

Colton, CA 92324-3052
315 N. La Cadena
(95¢/min., 24hrs.)
(900) 225-5222
($2.75/call) CC#
(909) 426-0813

Cypress, CA 90630-3966
6101 Ball Rd. Suite 309
(95¢/min., 24hrs.)
(900) 225-5222
($2.75/call) CC#
(909) 426-0813

Fresno, CA 93711
2519 W. Shaw #106
(209) 222-8111

**Los Angeles, CA
90020-2538**
3727 West 6th St., Suite 607
(95¢/min., 24hrs.)
(900) 225-5222
($2.75/call)CC#
(409) 926-0813

Monterey, CA 93940-2717
494 Alverado St., Suite C
(408) 372-3149

Oakland, CA 94612-1584
510 16th St., Suite 550
24hrs. (510) 238-1000

**Sacramento, CA
95814-6997**
400 S St.
(916) 443-6843

San Diego, CA 92123
5050 Murphy Canyon,
Ste. 110
24hrs. (619) 496-2131

San Francisco, CA 94104
114 Sansome St., Suite 1108
(415) 243-9999

San Jose, CA 95125
1530 Meridien Ave.,
Suite 100
(408) 445-3000

San Mateo, CA 94402-1706
400 S. El Camino Real,
Suite 350
P.O. Box 294
(94401-0294)
(415) 696-1240

Santa Barbara, CA 93102
213 Santa Barbara St.
P.O. Box 129 (93101)
(805) 963-8657

Stockton, CA 95202
11 S San Joaquin St.,
Suite 803
(209) 948-4880

Torrance, CA 90501
20280 S. Vermont, Suite 201
(310) 771-1447

Van Nuys, CA 91401
14532 Fria St., Suite A
(818) 374-4120

COLORADO

**Colorado Springs, CO
80907-5454**
3022 North El Paso
P.O. Box 7970
(80933-7970)
(719) 636-1155

Denver, CO 80222-4350
1780 S. Bellaire, Suite 700
(24hrs.) Inq.
(303) 758-2100

Fort Collins, CO 80525-1073
1730 S. College Ave.,
Suite 303
(303) 484-1348

Pueblo, CO 81003-3119
119 W. 6th St., Suite 203
(719) 542-6464

CONNECTICUT

**Wallingford, CT
06492-2420**
821 North Main Street Ext.
(203) 269-2700

DELAWARE

**Wilmington, DE
19802-5532**
1010 Concord Avenue
(302) 594-9200

DISTRICT OF COLUMBIA

**Washington, DC
20005-3410**
1012 14 St., NW, 9th Floor
(202) 393-8000

FLORIDA

Clearwater, FL 34620
5830-142nd Ave. N, Suite B
Pasco City (813) 842-5459
Pinellas City (813) 535-5522
Hills/Tampa
(813) 854-1154
Hernando (800) 525-1447
Sarasota/Manatee
(813) 957-0093

Fort Myers, FL 33901
2710 Swamp Cabbage Ct
(914) 275-4224

Jacksonville, FL 32211
7820 Arlington
Expressway, Suite 147
(904) 721-2288

**Pensacola, FL
32503-2533**
4900 Bayou Blvd., Ste. 112
P.O. Box 1511
(32597-1511)
(904) 494-0222

Port St. Lucie, FL
34954-5579
1950 Port St. Lucie Bvd.,
Suite 211
(407) 878-2010
(407) 337-2083

West Palm Beach, FL
33409
580 Village Blvd., Suite 340
(407) 686-2200
Martin City (407) 337-2083

Winter Park, FL
32789-1736 (Orlando)
1011 N. Wynmore Rd.,
Suite 204
(24 hrs.) (407) 621-3300

GEORGIA

Albany, GA 31701
101-1/2 S. Jackson, Ste #2
P.O. Box 808 (31702)
(912) 883-0744

Atlanta, GA
30303-3075
100 Edgewood Ave.,
Suite 1012
(404) 688-4910

Augusta, GA 30901
301 7th St.,
P.O. Box 2085
(30903-2085)
(706) 722-1574

Columbus, GA 31901
208 13th St.,
P.O. Box 2587 (31902)
(706) 324-0712,13

Macon, GA 31201
277 M.L.K. Blvd., Ste. 102
(912) 742-7999

Savannah, GA 314056
606 Abercorn Street,
Suite 108-C
(912) 354-7521

HAWAII

Honolulu, HI 96814-3801
1600 Kapiolani Blvd,.
Suite 201
(808) 942-2355

IDAHO

Boise, ID 83702-5320
1333 West Jefferson
(208) 342-4649

Idaho Falls, ID 83404-5926
1575 South Blvd.
(208) 523-9754

ILLINOIS

Chicago, IL 60611
330 N. Wabash Ave.,
Ste. 2006
($3.80/call) CC 3
(312) 832-0500
(95¢/min., 24 hrs.)
(900) 225-5222

Peoria, IL 61615-3770
3024 West Lake
(309) 688-3714

Rockford, IL 61104-1001
810 E. State St., 3rd Floor
($3.80/call) CC#
(815) 963-8967
(95¢/min., 24 hrs.)
(900) 225-5222

INDIANA

Elkhart, IN 46514-2988
722 W. Bristol Street,
Suite H-2
P.O. Box 405 (46515-0405)
(219) 262-8996

Evansville, IN 47715-2265
4004 Morgan Ave., Suite 201
(812) 473-0202, 1425

Fort Wayne, IN
46802-3493
1203 Webster St.
(219) 423-4433
NE IN only (800) 552-4631

Gary, IN 46408
4189 Cleveland St.
(219) 980-1511,
(219) 769-8053
219 area only
(800) 637-2118

Indianapolis, IN
46204-3584
Victoria Ctr., 22 E.
Washington St., Ste. 200
(317) 488-2222

South Bend, IN
46637-3360
207 Dixie Way North,
Suite 130
(219) 277-9121
No. IN only (800) 439-5313

IOWA

Bettendorf, IA
52722-4100
852 Middle Rd., Suite 290
(319) 355-6344

Des Moines, IA
50309-2375
505 5th Ave., Suite 615
(515) 243-8137

Sioux City, IA 51101
505 Sixth St., Suite 417
(712) 252-4501

KANSAS

Topeka, KS 6607-1190
501 Southeast Jefferson,
Suite 24
(913) 232-0454

Wichita, KS 67211
328 Laura
(316) 263-3146

KENTUCKY

Lexington. KY 40507-1616
410 W. Vine St., Suite 340
(24 hrs.) (606) 259-1008

Louisville, KY 40203-2186
844 S. Fourth St.
(24 hrs.) (502) 583-6546
(24 hrs.) S. IN & KY only
(800) 388-2222

LOUISIANA

Alexandria, LA 71301-6875
1605 Murray St., Suite 117
(318) 473-4494

**Baton Rouge, LA
70806-1546**
2055 Wooddale Boulevard
(504) 926-3010

Houma, LA 70364
953 West Park Ave., Ste. 4005
(504) 868-3456

Lafayette, LA 70506
100 Huggins Rd.
P.O. Box 30297
(70593-0297)
(318) 981-3497

Lake Charles, LA 70605
3941-L Ryan St.,
P.O. Box 7314
(70606-7314)
(318) 478-6253

Monroe, LA 71201-7380
141 Desiard St., Suite 808
(318) 387-4600

**New Orleans, LA
70130-5843**
1539 Jackson Ave., Ste 400
(24 hrs.) (504) 581-6222
(504) 528-9277

**Shreveport, LA
71105-2122**
3612 Youree Drive
(318) 868-5146

MAINE

**Portland, ME
04103-2648**
812 Stevens Avenue
(207) 878-2715

MARYLAND

Baltimore, MD 21211-3215
2100 Huntingdon Avenue
(95¢/min., 24 hrs.)
(900) 225-5222

MASSACHUSETTS

Boston, MA 02116
20 Park Plaza, Suite 820
(617) 426-9000
(802) area only
(800) 422-2811

**Springfield, MA
01103-1402**
293 Bridge St., Suite 320
(413) 734-3114

**Worcester, MA
01608-1900**
32 Franklin St.
P.O. Box 16555
(01601-6555)
(508) 755-2548

MICHIGAN

**Grand Rapids, MI
40503-3001**
40 Pearl St. NW,
Suite 354
(616) 774-8236
W. MI only (24 hrs.)
(800) 684-3222

**Southfield, MI
48076-7751 (Detroit)**
30555 Southfield Rd.,
Suite 200
(24 hrs.)(810) 644-9100

MINNESOTA

**Minneapolis-St. Paul
55116-2600**
2706 Gannon Road
(612) 699-1111
Complaint (800) 646-6222

MISSISSIPPI

Jackson, MS 39206
4500 I-55 North
P.O. Box 12745
(39236-2745)
(601) 987-8282

MISSOURI

**Kansas City, MO
64106-2418**
306 E. 12th St., Suite 1024
(816) 421-7800

St. Louis, MO 63110
12 Sunnen Drive, Suite 121
(24 hrs.) (314) 645-3300

**Springfield, MO
65806-1326**
205 Park Central East,
Suite 509
(417) 862-4222

NEBRASKA

Lincoln, NE 68510-1670
3633 'O' St., Suite 1
(402) 476-8855

Omaha, NE 68134-6022
2237 N. 91st Court
(402) 391-7612

NEVADA

**Las Vegas, NV
89104-1515**
1022 E. Sahara Ave.
(702) 735-6900

Reno, NV 89502
991 Bible Way
P.O. Box 21269
(89515-1269)
(702) 322-0657

NEW HAMPSHIRE

Concord, NH 03301-3483
410 Main St., Suite 3
(603) 224-1991
(603) 228-3789, 3844

NEW JERSEY

Parsippany, NJ 07054
(Newark)
400 Lanidex Plaza
(201)581-1313

Toms River, NJ
08753-8239
1721 Route 37 East
(908) 270-5577

Trenton, NJ 08960-3596
1700 Whitehorse-Hamilton
Sq., #D-5
(609) 588-0808

Westmont, NJ 08108-0303
16 Maple Ave., P.O. Box 303
(609) 854-8467

NEW MEXICO

Albuquerque, NM
87110-3657
2625 Pennsylvania NE,
Suite 2050
(505) 884-0500
NM only (800) 873-2224

Farmington, NM
87401-5855
308 North Locke
(505) 326-6501

Las Cruces, NM 88001-3548
201 N. Church, Suite 330
(505) 524-3130

NEW YORK

Buffalo, NY 14202
346 Delaware Ave.
($3.80/call) CC#
(716) 856-7180
(95¢/min., 24 hrs.)
(900) 225-5222

Farmingdale, NY 11735
266 Main St.
($3.80/call)
(212) 533-6200
(95¢/min., 24 hrs.)
(900) 225-5222

New York, NY 10010
257 Park Ave., South
($3.80/call) CC#
(212) 533-6200
(95¢/min., 24 hrs.)
(900) 225-5222

Syracuse, NY 13202
847 James St., Suite 200
($3.80/call) CC#
(716) 856-7180
(95¢/min., 24 hrs.)
(900) 225-5222

White Plains, NY 10603
30 Glenn St.
($3.80/call) CC#
(212) 533-6200
(95¢/min., 24 hrs.)
(900) 225-5222

NORTH CAROLINA

Asheville, NC
28801-3418
1200 BB&T Building
(704) 253-2392

Charlotte, NC 28209-3650
5200 Park Rd., Suite 202
(24 hrs.) (704) 527-0012

Greensboro, NC
27410-4895
3608 W. Friendly Ave.
(24 hrs.) (910) 852-4240

Raleigh, NC 27604-1080
3125 Poplarwood Ct.,
Suite 308
(919) 872-9240
East NC only
(800) 222-0950

Sherrills Ford, NC 28673
Eden Pl. 8366 Drena Dr.
P.O. Box 69 (28673-0069)
(704) 478-5622

Winston-Salem, NC
27101-2728
500 W. 5th St., Suite 202
(910) 725-8348

OHIO

Akron, OH 44303-2111
222 W. Market St.
(330) 253-4590

Canton, OH 44703-3135
1434 Cleveland Ave., NW
P.O. Box 8017
(44711-8017)
(330) 454-9401
OH only (800) 362-0494

Cincinnati, OH
45202-2097
898 Walnut St.
(513) 421-3015

Cleveland, OH 44115-1299
2217 East 9th St., Suite 200
(216) 241-7678

Columbus, OH 43215-1000
1335 Dublin, Suite 30A
(614) 486-6336

Dayton, OH 45402-1828
40 West Fourth St.,
Suite 1250
(937) 222-5825

Lima, OH 458802-0269
112N, N. West St. (45801)
P.O. Box 269
(419) 223-7010
(800) 462-0468

Toledo, OH 43604-1055
3103 Executive Pkwy, Ste. 200
(419) 531-3116

Youngstown, OH 44501-1495
600 Mahoning Bank Bldg.
P.O. Box 1495
(330) 744-3111
Lisbon (330) 424-5522
Warren (330) 394-0628

OKLAHOMA

**Oklahoma City, OK
73102-2400**
17 South Dewey
(405) 239-6081

Tulsa, OK 74136-3327
6711 South Yale, Suite 230
(918) 492-1266

OREGON

Portland, OR 97204
333 SW Fifth Ave., Suite 300
(610) 226-3981
OR/SW WA only
(800) 488-4155

PENNSYLVANIA

Bethlehem, PA 18018-5789
528 North New St.
(215) 866-8780
Berks Cty. (610) 372-2005

Lancaster, PA 17602-2852
29 E. King St., Suite 322
($3.80/call) CC#
(215) 448-3870
(95¢/min., 24 hrs.)
(900) 225-5222

Philadelphia, PA 19103-0297
1608 Walnut St, Suite 6.
($3.80/call) CC#
(215) 893-3870
(95¢/min., 24 hrs.)
(900) 225-5222

Pittsburgh, PA 15222-2511
300 Sixth Ave., Suite 100-UL
(412) 456-2700

Scranton, PA 18503-2204
129 N. Washington Ave.
P.O. Box 993
(18501-0993)
(717) 342-9129
(717) 655-0445

PUERTO RICO

San Juan, PR 009927-6100
1608 Bori St. (00926-3488)
P.O. Box 363488
(787) 756-5400

RHODE ISLAND

**Warwick, RI 02888-1071
(Providence)**
120 Lavan Street
Inq. (401) 785-1212
Comp. (401) 785-1213

SOUTH CAROLINA

Columbia, SC 29205
2330 Devine St.
P.O. Box 8326 (29201)
(803) 254-2525

Greenville, SC 29605-4077
307-B Falls Street
(864) 242-5052

**Myrtle Beach, SC
29577-1601**
1601 North Oak St.,
Suite 101
(803) 626-6881

TENNESSEE

**Blountville, TN
37617-1178**
777 Holston Dr., Ste. 205
P.O.Box 1178
(423) 325-6616

**Chattanooga, TN
37402-2614**
1010 Market St., Suite 200
(423) 266-6144

Knoxville, TN 37919
2633 Kingston Pike, Suite 2
P.O. Box 10327
(37939-0327)
(423) 522-2552

Memphis, TN 38120
6525 Quail Hollow,
Suite 410
P.O. Box 17036
(38187-0036)
24 hours (901) 759-1300

Murfreesboro, TN 37130
701 N. Walnut Street
(24 hrs.) (615) 242-4222

**Nashville, TN
37219-1778**
414 Union St., Ste. 1830
P.O. Box 198436
(37219-8436)
24 hours (615) 242-4222

TEXAS

Abilene, TX 79605-5052
3300 South 14th Street,
Suite 307
(915) 691-1533

**Amarillo, TX
79101-3408**
724 South Polk,
P.O. Box 1905
(79105-1905)
(806) 379-6222

Austin, TX 78741-3854
2101 South IH35, Suite 302
24 hours (512) 445-2911

**Beaumont, TX
77701-2011**
550 Fannin Street,
P.O. Box 2988
(77704-2988)
(409) 835-5348

Bryan, TX 77802-3868
4346 Carter Creek Pkwy
P.O. Box 3868 (77802)
(409) 260-2222

Corpus Christi, TX 78401
216 Park Ave.
(512) 887-4949

Dallas, TX 75201-3093
2001 Bryan St., Suite 850
($3.80/call) CC#
(214) 740-0348
(95¢/min., 24 hrs.)
(900) 225-5222

El Paso, TX 79901
Northwest Plaza, Ste. 1101
(24 hrs.) (915) 577-0191

Fort Worth, TX 76102-5978
1612 Summit Ave.,
Suite 260
(817) 332-7585

Houston, TX 77007
525 Katy Freeway, Ste. 500
($3.80/call) CC#
(713) 867-4946
(95¢/min., 24 hrs.)
(900) 225-5222

Lubbock, TX 79401-3410
916 Main St., Suite 800
(24 hrs.) (806) 763-0459

Midland, TX 79711-0206
10100 County Rd. -
118 West
P.O. Box 60206
(915) 563-1880
TX only (800) 592-4433

San Angelo, TX 76904
3121 Executive Drive
P.O. Box 3366
(76902-3366)
(915) 949-2989

San Antonio, TX 78217-5296
1800 Northeast Loop 410,
Suite 400
(210) 828-9441

Tyler, TX 75701
3600 Old Bullard Rd.,
Suite 103A
P.O. Box 6652
(75711-6652)
(903) 581-5704

Waco, TX 76710
6801 Sanger Ave., Suite 125
P.O. Box 7203
(76714-7203)
(817) 772-7530

Weslaco, TX 78599-0069
609 International Blvd.,
P.O. Box 69
(210) 968-3678

Wichita Falls, TX 76308-2830
4245 Kemp Blvd., Suite 900
(800) 388-1778

UTAH

Salt Lake City, UT 84115-5382
1588 South Main St.
(24 hrs.) (801) 487-4656
UT only (800) 456-3907

VERMONT

See Boston, MA
(802) area only
(800) 422-2811

VIRGINIA

Norfolk, VA 23509-1499
586 Virginian Drive
(757) 531-1300

Richmond, VA 23219-2332
701 East Franklin,
Suite 712
(24 hrs.) (804) 648-0016

Roanoke, VA 24011-1301
31 West Campbell Ave.
(540) 342-3455

WASHINGTON

Kennewick, WA 99336-3819
101 N. Union, #105
(509) 783-0892

Seatac, WA 98188
4800 South 188th St.,
Suite 222
P.O. Box 68926
($3.00) Inq./CC# ($2.00)
($4.00 Flat fee, 24 hrs.)
(900) 225-4222

Spokane, WA 99207-2356
508 W. Sixth Avenue,
Suite 401
(509) 455-4200

Yakima, WA 98901
32 No. 3rd St., Suite 410
P.O. Box 1584
(98907-1584)
(509) 248-1326

WISCONSIN

Milwaukee, WI 53203-2478
740 North Plankinton Ave.
Inq. (414) 273-1600
Comp. (414) 273-0123

International Bureaus (BBBs)

**Canadian
Council of
Better Business
Bureaus**

CALGARY, AB T2H 2H8
7330 Fisher Street, SE,
Suite 368
(403) 531-8686

ALBERTA

Calgary, AB V6B 2M1
7330 Fisher St., SE,
Suite 350
(403) 531-8780

Edmonton, AB T5K2L9
514 Capital Pl.
9707-110th St.
(403) 482-2341

BRITISH
COLUMBIA

Vancouver, BC V6B 2M1
788 Beatty St., Suite 404
(604) 682-2711

Victoria, BC V8W 1V7
201-1005 Langley St.
(604) 386-6348

MANITOBA

Winnepeg, MB R3B 2K3
301-365 Hargrave St.
(204) 943-1486

NEWFOUNDLAND

St. Johns, NF A1E 2B6
360 Topsail Rd.
(709) 364-2222

NOVA SCOTIA

Halifax, NS B3J 3B8
1888 Brunswick St.,
Suite 601
Inq. (902) 422-6581
Comp. (902) 422-6582

ONTARIO

Hamilton, ON L8N 1A8
100 King St., East
(905) 526-1112

Kitchener, ON N2G 4L5
354 Charles St., East
(519) 579-3080

London, ON N2A 1J3
200 Queens Ave., Suite 616
P.O. Box 2153 (N6A 4E3)
(519) 673-3222

Ottawa, ON K1P 5N2
130 Albert St., Suite 603
(613) 237-4856

St. Catherines, ON L2R 3H6
101 King St.
(905) 687-6688

Toronto, ON M6P 4C7
One St. John's Rd., Suite 501
(416) 766-5744

Windsor, ON N9A 5K6
500 Riverside Dr. West
(519) 258-7222

QUEBEC

Montreal, PQ H3A 1V4
2055 Peel St., Suite 460
(514) 286-9281

Quebec City, PQ G1R 1K2
485 rue Richelieu
(418) 523-2555

SASKATCHEWAN

Regina, SA S4P 1Y3
302-2080 Broad St.
(306) 352-7601

*CC# = Call charged to
Consumer's credit card.

Better Business Bureaus Annual Statistics

Investment-Related Businesses: INQUIRY Statistics

TYPE OF BUSINESS	1995	1996	%Change
Business Opportunity Companies	59,058	90,568	53.4%
Commodities Brokers and Dealers	1,439	2,780	93.2%
Financial Advisory Services/Business Consultants	40,186	55,190	37.3%
Financial/Investment Companies & Services	23,837	21,262	-10.8%
Franchise/Business Promotions	7,628	8,114	6.4%
Investment and Business Brokers/Dealers	10,029	18,683	86.3%
Land Development Companies/Real Estate	5,769	4,972	-13.8%
Multi-Level Selling Companies	45,062	77,180	71.3%
Oil and Gas Leases and Lotteries	661	1,854	180.5%
Ponzis and Pyramids	2,518	7,247	187.8%
Securities Brokers and Dealers	15,232	8,977	-41.1%
Timeshare/Resort Promotions	38,091	30,730	-19.3%
TOTAL	**249,510**	**327,557**	**31.3%**

Investment-Related Businesses: COMPLAINT Statistics

TYPE OF BUSINESS	1995	1996	%Change
Business Opportunity Companies	726	1,226	95.7%
Commodities Brokers and Dealers	26	28	7.7%
Financial Advisory Services/Business Consultants	434	549	26.5%
Financial/Investment Companies & Services	302	525	73.8%
Franchise/Business Promotions	151	152	0.7%
Investment and Business Brokers/Dealers	94	198	110.6%
Land Development Companies/Real Estate	206	193	-6.3%
Multi-Level Selling Companies	254	1,039	309.1%
Oil and Gas Leases and Lotteries	34	62	82.4%
Ponzis and Pyramids	9	33	266.7%
Securities Brokers and Dealers	89	115	29.2%
Timeshare/Resort Promotions	1,045	795	-23.9%
TOTAL	**3,370**	**4,915**	**45.8%**

In 1996, BBBs nationwide received 327,000 investment-related inquires, a 31% increase over the prior year. The number of complaints filed with BBBs against various investment-related businesses rose 46% between 1995 to 1996.

The North American Securities Administrators Association is an organization comprised of all state, territorial, and provincial securities administrators in the United States, Canada, and Mexico who are charged with enforcing their jurisdictions' securities laws and protecting the public from fraudulent investments.

North American Securities Administrators Association, Inc.

One Massachusetts Avenue, NW, Suite 310
Washington, DC 20001
(202) 737-0900 Fax (202) 783-3571
World Wide Web: http://www.nasaa.org

Alabama
Securities Commission
770 Washington Avenue
Suite 570
Montgomery, AL 36130-4700
(334) 242-2984

Alaska
Dept. of Commerce and
Economic Development
Division of Banking,
Securities, & Corporations
P.O. Box 110807
Juneau, AK 99811-0807
(907) 465-2521

Alberta
Securities Commission
300-5th Avenue SW,
4th Floor
Calgary, Alberta
T2P 3C4
(403) 297-6454

Securities Commission
10025 Jasper Avenue
19th Floor

Edmonton, Alberta
T5J 3Z5 CANADA
(403) 427-5201

Arizona
Corporation Commission
Securities Division
1300 West Washington St.,
Third Floor
Phoenix, AZ 85007
(602) 542-4242

Arkansas
Securities Department
Heritage West Building
201 East Markham, 3rd Floor
Little Rock, AR 72201
(501) 324-9260

British Columbia
Securities Commission
865 Hornby St., 11th Floor
Vancouver, British Columbia
V6Z 2H4 CANADA
(604) 660-4800

California
Department of Corporations

3700 Wilshire Boulevard
Suite 600
Los Angeles, CA 90010
(213) 736-2741

Colorado
Division of Securities
1580 Lincoln, Suite 420
Denver, CO 80203
(303) 894-2320

Connecticut
Department of Banking
Securities & Business
Investments Division
260 Constitution Plaza
Hartford, CT 06103
(860) 240-8230

Delaware
Department of Justice
Division of Securities
State Office Building
820 N. French Street,
8th Floor
Wilmington, DE 19801
(302) 577-8424

District of Columbia
Securities Commission
717 14th Street NW
Suite 300
Washington, DC 20005
(202) 626-5105

Florida
Office of Comptroller
Department of Banking and
Finance
Plaza Level, The Capitol
Tallahassee, FL 32399-0350
(904) 488-9805

Georgia
Office of the Secretary of State
Division of Business Services
and Regulation
2 Martin Luther King Dr.
802 West Tower
Atlanta, GA 30334
(404) 656-2894

Hawaii
Department of Commerce &
Consumer Affairs
P.O. Box 40
Honolulu, HI 96810
(808) 586-2744

Idaho
Department of Finance
Securities Bureau
P.O. Box 83720
Boise, ID 83720-0031
(208) 332-8004

Illinois
Office of Secretary of State
Securities Department
Lincoln Tower
Suite 200
520 South 2nd Street
Springfield, IL 62701
(217) 782-2256

Indiana
Office of the Secretary of State
Securities Division
302 West Washington
Room E-111
Indianapolis, IN 46204
(317) 232-6681

Iowa
Insurance Division
Securities Bureau
321 East 12th Street
Lucas State Office Building
Des Moines, IA 50319
(515) 281-4441

Kansas
Office of the Securities
Commissioner
618 South Kansas Avenue
2nd Floor
Topeka, KS 66603-3804
(913) 296-3307

Kentucky
Department of Financial
Institutions
Division of Securities
477 Versailles Road
Frankfort, KY 40601
(502) 573-3390

Louisiana
Securities Commission
Energy Centre
1100 Poydras Street
Suite 2250
New Orleans, LA 70163
(504) 568-5515

Maine
Dept. of Professional &
Financial Regulation
Bureau of Banking
Securities Division
State House Station 121
Augusta, ME 04333
(207) 624-8551

Manitoba
Securities Commission
1128-405 Broadway
Winnipeg, Manitoba
R3C-3LC CANADA
(204) 945-2548

Maryland
Office of the Attorney General
Division of Securities
200 St. Paul Place, 20th Floor
Baltimore, MD
21202-2020
(410) 576-6360

Massachusetts
Secretary of the
Commonwealth
Securities Division
One Ashburton Place,
Room 1701
Boston, MA 02108
(617) 727-3548

Mexico
Comision Nacional de
Valores
Av. Insergentes
Sur 1971
Torre Sur, Piso 10
Col. Guadelupe Inn C.P.
01020
011-525-661-5483

Michigan
Department of Commerce
Corporation and Securities
Bureau
6546 Mercantile Way
Lansing, MI 48910
(517) 334-6212

Minnesota
Department of Commerce
133 East Seventh Street
St. Paul, MN 55101
(612) 296-4026

Mississippi
Office of the Secretary of State
Securities Division
P.O. Box 136
Jackson, MS 39205
(601) 359-6371

Missouri
Office of the Secretary
of State
600 W. Main Street
Jefferson City, MO
65101
(573) 751-4136

Montana
Office of the State Auditor
Securities Department
P.O. Box 4009
Helena, MT 59604
(406) 444-2040

Nebraska
Department of Banking and
Finance
Bureau of Securities
P.O. Box 95006
Lincoln, NE 68509
(402) 471-3445

Nevada
Office of the Secretary of State
Securities Division
555 E. Washington Ave, 5 Fl,
Suite 5200
Las Vegas, NV 89101
(702) 486-2440

New Brunswick
Securities Branch
P.O. Box 5001
St. John, New Brunswick
E2L 4Y9 CANADA
(506) 658-3060

Newfoundland
Department of Justice
Securities Division
P.O. Box 8700
St. Johns, Newfoundland
AIB 4J6 Canada
(709) 729-4189

New Hampshire
Bureau of Securities
Regulation
Department of State

State House, Room 204
Concord, NH 03301-4989
(603) 271-1463

New Jersey
Department of Law & Public
Safety
Bureau of Securities
153 Halsey St.
P.O. Box 47029
Newark, NJ 07101
(201) 504-3600

New Mexico
Regulation and Licensing
Department
Securities Division
725 St. Michaels Dr.
Santa Fe, NM 87501
(505) 827-7140

New York
Department of Law
Bureau of Investor Protection
& Securities
120 Broadway, 23rd Floor
New York, NY 10271
(212) 416-8200

North Carolina
Office of the Secretary of State
Securities Division
300 North Salisbury Street
Suite 301
Raleigh, NC 27603-5909
(919) 733-3924

North Dakota
Office of the Securities
Commissioner
State Capitol; 5th Floor
600 East Boulevard
Bismarck, ND 58505
(701) 328-2910

Northwest Territories
Securities Registry
Government of the Northwest
Territories
4903 49th Street

Yellowknife, Northwest
Territories X1A 2L9 CANADA
(403) 873-7490

Nova Scotia
Securities Commission
1690 Hollis Street
2nd Floor, Jospeh Howe
Building
Halifax, Nova Scotia
B3J 2P8 CANADA
(902) 424-7768

Ohio
Division of Securities
77 South High Street
22nd Floor
Columbus, OH 43215
(614) 644-7381

Oklahoma
Division of Securities
First National Center
120 N. Robinson St., Suite 860
Oklahoma City, OK 73102
(405) 280-7700

Ontario
Securities Commission
20 Queen Street West
Suite 1800
Toronto, Ontario
M5H 3S8 CANADA
(416) 597-0681

Oregon
Department of Insurance and
Finance
Division of Finance &
Corporate Securities
350 Winter, NE, Rm. 410
Salem, OR 97310
(503) 378-4387

Pennsylvania
Securities Commission
Eastgate Office Building
1010 North 7th St., 2nd Fl
Harrisburg, PA 17102-1410
(717) 787-8061

Prince Edward Island
Department of Justice;
Securities Act
95 Rochford Street; 4th Floor
Charlottetown, Prince Edward
Island
C1A-7N8 CANADA
(902) 368-4552

Puerto Rico
Office of the Commissioner of
Financial Institutions
Government Employees
Centro Europa Building
1492 Ponce de Leon Avenue,
Suite 600
San Juan, Puerto Rico
00907-4127
(809) 751-5606, 7837

Quebec
Commission des valeurs
mobiliers du Quebec
800 Square Victoria, 17th Flr.
P.O. Box 246
Stock Exchange Tower
Montreal, Quebec
H4Z 1G3 CANADA
(514) 873-5326

Rhode Island
Department of Business
Regulation
Securities Division
233 Richmond Street,
Suite 232
Providence, RI 02903-4232
(401) 277-3048

Saskatchewan
Securities Commission
Suite 800
1920 Broad Street
Regina, Saskatchewan
S4P-3V7 CANADA
(306) 787-5645

South Carolina
Department of State
Securities Division

1000 Assembly Street
Columbia, SC 29202
(803) 734-1807

South Dakota
Division of Securities
118 West Capitol Avenue
Pierre, SD 57501-2017
(605) 773-4823

Tennessee
Department of Commerce &
Insurance Securities Division
Davy Crockett Tower
Suite 680
500 James Robertson
Parkway
Nashville, TN 37243-0575
(615) 741-2947

Texas
State Securities Board
P.O. Box 13167
Austin, TX 78711-3167
(512) 305-8300

Utah
Department of Commerce
Securities Division
Box 146760
Salt Lake City, UT
84114-6760
(801) 530-6600

Vermont
Department of Banking,
Insurance & Securities
Securities Division
89 Main Street, 2nd Floor
Montpelier, VT 05620-3101
(802) 828-3420

Virginia
State Corporation
Commission
Division of Securities &
Retail Franchising
1300 E. Main Street, 9th floor
Richmond, VA 23219

Washington
Department of Financial
Institutions
Securities Division
P.O. Box 9033
Olympia, WA 98507-9033
(360) 902-87660

West Virginia
State Auditor's Office
Securities Division
State Capitol Building
Building 1, Room W-114
Charleston, WV 25305
(304) 558-2257

Wisconsin
Division of Securities
P.O. Box 1768
Madison, WI
53701-1768
(608) 251-9555

Wyoming
Secretary of State
Securities Division
State Capitol Building,
Room 109
200 W. 24th Street
Cheyenne, WY
82002-0020
(307) 777-7370

Yukon Territory
Department of Justice
Justice Services Division
Corporate Affairs
P.O. Box 2703
Whitehorse, Yukon
Y1A 2C6 CANADA
(403) 667-5225

North American Securities Administrators Association (NASAA)

ENFORCEMENT ACTIONS 1995-1996		
	1995	**1996**
Investigations Initiated	6,035	6,840
Cease and Desist Orders Issued	1,245	1,189
Denials, Suspensions and Revocations of Securities Dealers/Salespersons and Investment Advisers/Investment Adviser Representatives Licences	690	1,122
Permanent and Temporary Injunctions Granted by Courts	223	172
Criminal Proceedings Initiated	326	325
Criminal Convictions	195	236
Consent Orders	654	750
Amounts Offered or Returned to Investors from Settlements	$38,395,472.23	$85,686,886.57

Enforcement activity was on the upswing during this time period. These enforcement statistics were compiled from survey responses of NASAA U.S. members. Not all U.S. members responded to the surveys since their enforcement action totals were not readily available. For 1995, fifteen U.S. NASAA members' enforcement actions are not included in all categories, and for 1996, three U.S. members' actions are not included in these totals.

The following list provides addresses and phone numbers for agencies and organizations referred to in this publication. A sketch of the areas of activity of each organization, as it relates to our topic, follows in italics.

The names, addresses, phone numbers, and office descriptions presented here have been thoroughly checked. However, because of changes that may take place after publication, some information may no longer be current. We regret any inconvenience this may cause.

American Gemological Laboratories
Gemline Recovery Service
580 5th Avenue—Room 706
New York, NY 10036
(212) 704-0727
(800) 862-4272
questions involving possible fraud or misrepresentation in gem dealings

American Gem Society—
NO LISTINGS
verifying membership of gem dealers; list of dealers in your area; guidelines for buying gems and jewelry

American Institute of Certified Public Accountants
1211 Avenue of the Americas
New York, NY 10036
(212) 596-6200
(800) 862-4272
confirming qualification of CPAs

Commodity Futures Trading Commission (CFTC)
3 Lafayette Center
1155 21st Street NW
Washington, DC 20581
(202) 418-5000
(800) 862-4272

information regarding commodity futures trading; verifying licensing and complaint history of commodities firms.

REGIONAL CFTC OFFICES

Chicago
300 Riverside Plaza
Suite1600 N
Chicago, IL 60606
(312) 886-9000

Kansas City
4900 Main Street
Suite 721
Kansas City, MO 64112
(816) 931-7600

Los Angeles
10980 Wilshire Boulevard
Suite 400
Los Angeles, CA 90024
(310) 235-6783

Minneapolis
510 Grain Exchange Building
Minneapolis, MN 55415
(612) 370-3255

New York
One World Trade Center
Suite 3747
New York, NY 10048
(212) 466-2017

Direct Selling Association
1666 K. Street NW
Suite 1010
Washington, DC 20006
(202) 293-5760
verifying membership of companies involved in direct sales

Federal Trade Commission (FTC)
6th Street & Pennsylvania Ave., NW
Washington, DC 20580
(202) 326-2000
questions involving deceptive business practices

REGIONAL FTC OFFICES

Atlanta
1718 Peachtree Street
Suite 1000
Atlanta, GA 30367
(404) 347-4836

Boston
101 Merrimack Street
Suite 810
Boston, MA 02114-4719
(617) 424-5960

Chicago
55 East Monroe St.,
Suite 1437
Chicago, IL 60603
(312) 353-4423

Cleveland
668 Euclid Avenue
Suite 520-A
Cleveland, OH
44114
(216) 522-4207
(216) 522-4210

Dallas
100 N. Central
Expressway
Suite 500
Dallas, TX 75201
(214) 979-0213

Denver
1405 Curtis Street
Suite 2900
Denver, CO 80202-2393
(303) 844-2271

Los Angeles
11000 Wilshire Blvd.
Los Angeles, CA 90024
(310) 235-7890

New York
150 William Street
13th Floor
New York, NY 10038
(212) 264-1207

San Francisco
901 Market Street
Suite 570
San Francisco, CA
94103
(415) 356-5270

Seattle
2806 Federal Building
915 Second Ave.
Seattle, WA 98174
(206) 220-6363

**Housing and Urban
Development Department
(HUD)**
Community Planning &
Development
HUD Building
451 7th Street, SW,
Room 7100
Washington, DC 20410-
8000
(202) 708-2690
*verifying land sales regis-
tration; information regard-
ing complaint history*

**Institute of
Certified Financial
Planners**
3801 East Florida Street
Suite 708
Denver, CO 80231
(303) 759-4900
(800) 282-7526
*information on how to
select a financial planner;
list of Certified Financial
Planners in your area*

**International
Association for Financial
Planning**
Two Concourse Parkway
Suite B-300
Atlanta, GA 30328-5364
(800) 945-4237
*verifying membership of
financial planners; list of
financial planners in your
area*

**International
Foundation for Art
Research**
500 5th Avenue
Suite 1234
New York, NY 10021
(212) 391-6234
*general guidelines for pur-
chasing art; authentication
services*

**National Association of
Home Builders**
1201 15th St., NW
Washington, DC 20006
(202) 822-0200
*general guidelines for buy-
ing a home; information on
your local homebuilders
association*

**National Association of
Personal Financial
Advisors**
355 West Dunde Road
Suite 200
Buffalo Grove, IL 60089
(847) 537-7722
(888) 333-6659
*verifying membership of
financial advisors, list of
fee-only financial advisors
in your area*

**National Association of
Securities Dealers (NASD)**
1735 K St., NW
Washington, DC 20006
(202) 728-8000
Consumer Hotline
(800) 289-9999
*verifying membership of
securities dealers; assistance with complaints*

**National Futures
Association (NFA)**
200 West Madison St.
Suite 1600
Chicago, IL 60606
(800) 572-9400—Illinois
Residents
(800) 621-3570—Outside
Illinois
*verifying registration of
commodities firms/dealers;
information regarding any
NFA disciplinary actions;
assistance in arbitrating
claims; questions involving
investors' rights.*

Professional Coin Grading Service
P.O. Box 9458
Newport Beach, CA 92658
1-800-447-8848
  list of authorized dealers

Securities Exchange Commission (SEC)
450 5th St., NW
Washington, DC 20549
(202) 942-8088
Consumer Hotline
1-800-SEC-0330
  information on public stock issues and securities fraud; verifying registration of securities brokers and investment advisers

REGIONAL SEC OFFICES

Atlanta
Suite 1000
3475 Lenox Rd., NE
Atlanta, GA 30326
(404) 842-7600

Boston
J.W. McCormick Post Office & Court House Building
73 Tremont St., Suite 600
Boston, MA 02108-3912
(617) 424-5900

Chicago
Suite 1400
Northwestern Atrium Center
500 W. Madison St.
Chicago, IL 60661
(312) 353-7390

Denver
1801 California St.
Denver, CO 80202-2648
(303) 391-6800

Fort Worth
801 Cherry Street
19th Floor
Fort Worth, TX 76102
(817) 978-3821

Los Angeles
5650 Wilshire Boulevard
11th Floor
Los Angeles, CA 90036-3648
(213) 965-3998

Miami
1401 Brickell Ave.
Suite 200
Miami, FL 3331131
(305) 536-4700

New York
13th Floor
7 World Trade Center
New York, NY 10048
(212) 748-8000

Philadelphia
The Curtis Center
Suite 1005 E
601 Walnut St.
Philadelphia, PA 19106-3322
(215) 597-3100

Salt Lake City
50 S. Main St., Suite 500
Salt Lake City, UT 84144-0402
(801) 524-5796

San Francisco
44 Montgomery St.,
Suite 1100
San Francisco, CA 94104
(415) 705-2500

Securities Investor Protection Corporation (SIPC)
805 15th St. NW
Suite 800
Washington, DC 20005-2207
(202) 371-8300
  verifying membership of brokers and dealers

United States Bureau of Land Management
18th & C Streets, NW
Washington, DC 20240
(202) 208-5717
  information regarding land auctions; oil and gas leasing

United States Postal Service
Chief Postal Inspector
Fraud Section
475 L'Enfant Plaza West, SW
Washington, DC 20260
(202) 268-2000
  reporting any phony invoices or other fraud involving documents sent through the U.S. mail

INDEX

General partnership, 69
Gifting network, 105
Griffin, Mark, 115, 116, 158-159

High-tech scams
application mill, 49
cautionary tips for, 56-59
interactive video and data service, 55-56
licenses and lotteries, 48-50
paging license scams, 53-55
pay-per-call 900-number scams, 56
specialized mobile radio, 52-53
wireless cable television, 50-52

Infomercials, "IRA-approved" investment schemes and, 68
Interactive video and data service (IVDS), 55-56, 67
International Franchise Association, 15
International investments
Bre-X gold scam, 80
foreign lottery scams, 74, 81
Nigerian prince scam, 78-79
prime bank guarantee scams, 73-74, 81
pyramid schemes, 76
risks of, 72
scams on Internet, 75
telemarketing fraud and, 75-76, 116-118
tips for, 77-81
unregistered and falsely represented securities, 76
Internet. *See also* On-line investment fraud
BBBOnline Program, 136
Better Business Bureau web site, 5, 9, 134, 135-136
Council of Better Business Bureaus web site, 135-136
foreign investment fraud on, 75
fraud on, 4
National Association of Securities Dealers web site, 134, 136-137
National Fraud and Information Center web site, 134

North American Securities Administrators Association web site, 5, 9, 134, 137
pyramids and, 105-106
Securities and Exchange Commission web site, 134
Invention marketing schemes, 20
Investments
investigate before, 6-8
overseeing your, 163-165
precautions related to religious communities, 146-147
prevalence of fraud, 4
Investment advisers
registration of, 148
unethical brokers on Internet, 130
Investment Advisers Act, 148
Investors
becoming informed, 9-10
Bill of Rights: Commodities, 30
checklist for starting point, 8
do's and don'ts for, 10-11
"IRA-approved" investment schemes, 61-69
diversity of, 66-68
self-defense tips for, 64-65
tips and precautions for, 68-69
IRS, IRA-approved investment, 66, 68

Junk bonds, 40-41

Limited liability company, 69
Limited partnerships, real estate, 90-91
Lottery scams, foreign, 74

Mugs Plus, Inc., 115

National Association of Securities Dealers, 160
Over-the-Counter Bulletin Board for penny stock, 42
telephone information retrieval system, 136-137
web site, 134, 136-137
National Fraud and Information Center, web site, 134
National Futures Association, 30
phone number for, 34

National Quotation Bureau, Inc., 41
Nigerian prince scam, 78-79
North American Securities Administrators Association telephone information retrieval system, 5, 9
web site, 5, 9, 134, 137

On Line Communications, 54
On-line investment fraud, 124-137. *See also* Internet
advantages of using Internet for, 127-128
examples of, 126-127
exotic scams, 130-131
investment adviser misconduct, 130
NASAA web page, 136-137
pump and dump scams, 128-130
pyramid schemes, 128-129
tips to prevent, 132-135
unregistered sales of securities, 131-132
Operation Disconnect, 114
Operation Missed Fortune, 18-19
Operation Senior Sentinel, 115

Paging license scams, 53-55
Pay-per-call 900-number scams, 56
Penny stock
ask price for, 44
bid price for, 44
characteristics of, 40-41
fraud, 40-45
Over-the-Counter Bulletin Board for, 42
pink sheets, 41
prices of, 41-42
pump and dump, 42
risk disclosure document, 44
suitability statement for, 43
tips and precautions for, 43-45
Phone card sales, 104-105
Pink sheets, 41
Ponzi, Charles, 97-98
Ponzi schemes, 7, 95-106
origin of, 97-98
vs. pyramid, 102
rules to avoid, 101-102
variations on, 98-100